THE G-SALE BIBLE

YOUR COMPLETE GUIDE TO HOLDING AND/OR FINDING THE WORLD'S GREATEST GARAGE SALE

KIMBERLY FOSTER

Introduction...5

Do I really need a Garage Sale Bible? 7

Chapter 1. Sellers, What's your motivation? 9

    Show me the money sale 14

    The "It's all Gotta GO NOW!" Sale.........................21

Chapter 2. Get the Lingo Down 27

    What's in a name: 27

    Estate Sales...27

    There's an app for that!...31

    The Yard Sale..31

    Moving Sales 33

    The Multi-Family Sale 35

    The Neighborhood Sale..36

    The Garage Sale 37

Chapter 3. Know Your Audience 40

    What do I have for Sale 40

    Inventory your items 42

    Who's going to buy my stuff?...................................44

    What if I don't have a Theme?..................................45

Chapter 4. Pricing the Priceless......................................47

    Personal Value vs. Actual Value...............................49

    Pricing Exercise...53

    Pricing Strategies...60

Chapter 5. Advertising...75

    Online/Digital Advertising 77

Chapter 6. What NOT to Sell at your Sale 89

Donate your clothes and sell your stuff............................... 90

Bits and Bobs... 92

Chapter 7. Let's Talk about the Weather 99

A Sale for all Seasons.. 100

Bring the party indoors.. 104

Chapter 8. Planning the Layout 109

Business in the front, Party in the back.......................... 109

My Garage Sale Layout 112

Kiddieland 113

Chapter 9. Permits, Licenses and Fees, OH MY!....................... 116

Do I need a Permit?.. 117

How do I find out if I need a permit? 117

What if the cost for the permit is too high? 121

Better to ask for forgiveness than permission 123

Chapter 10. Ok Sale-ers, Let's get Sale-ing............................... 125

what's your motivation?.. 125

Stick Close to Home or Jack Kerouac it.............................. 127

You want HOW Much?.. 130

Sale-ing with Friends 140

Pricing Tool.. 142

Garage sale Layout tools... 143

Bonus: How to Organize a Neighborhood Sale 145

Local government approval and buy-in 147

Agreed Upon Date 147

Participating Neighbors List.. 148

Communication and Advertising 149

Local Business Buy-in... 152

Larger Purpose Sale.. 153

After Sale Clean-Up 154

Let's talk funding 157

Neighborhood Garage Sale Wrap Party.................... 159

Final thoughts for Organizers..................................... 160

Other Books By Kimberly Foster 162

One Last Thing... 163

INTRODUCTION

I wrote this book as a guide for both sellers and "sale-ers". For Sellers, this manual offers instructions on how to put on a spectacularly profitable sale. I've researched the best sales as well as the not-so-great sales. I've surveyed profitable and flat-lined sale results and I've hit on some tips and tricks guaranteed to help you whether you're buying or selling.

In my life, I've furnished entire homes with G-sale finds. Now people tend to use online classifieds to sell items that would normally be found at garage sales. Some ads even go so far as to call themselves Online Garage Sales. This method makes a lot of sense but it can also limit the audience. Additionally, there are huge advantages to flinging open the garage door and letting the world in. Passing traffic, negotiating deals, impulse buying or just simply meeting your neighbors are just a few of the reasons garage sales are much more fun and profitable than posting online. But I don't discount the online option. In this book you'll learn how to use free online options to drive traffic to your real world sale.

For "Sale-ers": Garage sale-ing is so much fun! As a hobby, I've been garage sale-ing for forty years. Personally, I can't think of a better way to spend a Saturday than to go to the neighborhood sales and find treasures or complete junk at ridiculously cheap prices. But finding great sales isn't easy. In fact, lately I've found it can be next to impossible. I wrote this book to improve your odds of finding that amazing sale. I've made all the mistakes both in trying to hold a sale and finding good sales and I've compiled the right way to do it here.

I hope that you find this book helpful and I can come and buy all your stuff.

Do I really need a Garage Sale Bible?

The G-Sale Bible ....

1) Saves you time

For Sale-ers: Garage sale-ing can be a fantastic way to spend the day or a dismal waste of time. This book offers ways to increase the odds of a profitable day out. For Sellers: the guide offers tips and tricks to avoid putting on a time wasting sale. For Sale-ers, there's nothing worse that missing out on something a block away because you were visiting a sale with nothing to offer. For Sellers, there's nothing worse than sitting all day and watching potential customers walking past your sale rolling their eyes at your offerings. G-Sale bible will help you avoid the pitfalls of the time waster sale.

2) Saves you money

The G-Sale Bible will help you curtail your expenses. Garage sales can be costly. For Sellers; advertising, permits and energy are just some of the costs that go into conducting a sale. For Sale-ers, driving around to sale after sale without finding the deals isn't exactly cost effective and doesn't really help the environment either. It's no good to find a crock pot for $5 if you spent $30 in gas to get it. The bible helps you define your budget and spend wisely.

3) Helps you determine what to sell/buy

The G-Sale Bible gives you tips on what sells and what does not. Additionally, the bible helps you determine pricing both as a seller and as a buyer. The bible offers some straight talk about pricing and motivation.

Chapter 1. Sellers, What's your motivation?

This seems like a silly question on the surface. Clearly if you're reading this book, your motivation is to have a successful sale. But what I'm really asking is what is your desired result or outcome from your sale? For years I've said there are only two kinds of garage sales; ones trying to make money and ones trying to get rid of stuff. Sellers often are hoping for the former and end up praying for the latter. Sale-ers are always hoping for the latter but end up at the former more times than not.

Why is this important? Besides managing expectations, the key to successful selling and sale-ing is knowing what you want to achieve and being very rational about what steps will be required to achieve your goal. If you are immovable on price, whether you are a seller or sale-er, you will have a difficult time achieving your goal. Any item up for sale is only worth what the market will bear. Likewise, Sale-ers need to be mindful on the value of an item before making an offer.

I went to a garage sale, about two months ago, the garage sales in my neighborhood are typically dreadful and a big inspiration for this book, but this one sale had some potential.

First, let me explain, I am a tool geek. I love tools. Power tools in particular. When I got my first DeWalt I was almost giddy with excitement. This garage sale had Ryobi cordless tools. Now I'm a DeWalt girl but I will cheat with Ryobi if the price is right. There was a blue canvas bag of Ryobi (rather dirty and dusty) power tools and the woman said she just wanted to get rid of them. That's what I like to hear! She had a number of different tools, most of which I already have but a couple of things I thought would be nice to add to my collection. Particularly, there was a battery chainsaw, which I was very excited to see. Only problem with this bag o' tools was that the batteries were the old NiCad. If you don't know, these batteries degrade over time and are useless after a few years. Nowadays, Lithium-ion batteries have displaced NiCad. Lithium batteries are lighter, last longer (lifetime) and are more environmentally friendly. Also, none of her batteries were charged so I couldn't really test the tools themselves. I was willing to take the chance for the right price. She said she wanted $100 for them. On the surface this isn't a bad price, there was a lot of tools in the bag. But by the same token, $100 was a bit of a risk on a bag of dirty tools you can't test.

Sellers, here's an important side-lesson; As I'm writing this, it's 2018, no one carries cash anymore. I'm a Sale-er so I am carrying some cash for Sale-ing but NOT $100.

As she said she wanted to get rid of them and because I did want them despite their condition, I reviewed my cash on hand to see what offer I could make. I had $47 in cash. That's quite a lot for me but I knew I'd be sale-ing. I offered this to her and she refused it. She looked a little indignant, so I tried to reassure her that I wasn't insulting her. This was simply what I had and what I'd be willing to give her for tools that may or may not work.

She refused the offer and I walked away. Sale-ers, this is a critical lesson for you as well. You have to be able to walk away from a deal. It's not easy; obviously since I'm still thinking about that bag of tools. But the bottom-line will always be price. The biggest mistake Sale-ers make is not assessing the value of an item and then sticking to that price.

As it was, the price of the tools seemed reasonable to me on the surface. Then I started to analyze, "How much life is left in those NiCad's? What if half the tools don't work? Where am I going to find a replacement NiCad that won't cost me more than the tool is worth? Is it worth the risk? Hmmmm, not at $100. I think the most I'll pay is $60." This was my thought process, I assessed what I would be willing to pay. I hadn't realized I only had $47 at the time and I offered what I had. Had she countered with $60, I would have gotten the extra money. Had she countered with $80, I would have said no. The only time you should consider a higher counter is if it fits within your estimation of the item's value. There's nothing worse than paying more for something than you feel it was worth. Listen to your gut. You may find something that you are absolutely crazy about but there's a little voice in you saying, "Gosh, I just love it! The price does seem high though." Listen to the voice. If you pay the asking price, when you get it home the price will always be a part of the story. "I saw that vase and I just had to have it. I paid too much for it but I got it." Motivation for Sale-ers is just as critical as it is for Sellers. Know what you want before you go out. Know what you're willing to pay for what you want and don't waiver. If you don't find what you're looking for, move on to the next sale or try another tack but stay on target.

Sellers, the mistake the woman made was not making a counter offer. I may have taken it. I would have had to go get more money, but I would have responded to a price of $60. Can you guess what this seller's motivation was?

The biggest lesson from this experience is that no one was happy. The seller didn't make money and I didn't get what I wanted. While she said she wanted to get rid of the tools, in reality she wanted her asking price. This is a real pet peeve for a lot of Sale-ers I talk to and one of mine as well. Be clear about your goal and act accordingly. If it's about the money, own it. If it's about getting rid of stuff, show it. Decide what you want and work towards the goal. If you don't think an offer is reasonable, then by all means make a counter offer, but if you say you want to get rid of something and yet refuse an offer to achieve this goal, you just ended any chance of success.

Every interaction at your garage sale should result in two happy parties, the seller and the sale-er. If that's not happening, then your sale is unsuccessful.

UPDATE....UPDATE....UPDATE

Since writing this a few months ago, I've got an update to the story of the bag o' tools.

For the past two weeks, I've been dealing with a water heater issue. Oh, I could just scream. I bought a water heater at a popular home improvement store less than 4 years ago and it died. I spent over $200 to get it fixed and it died again a week later. I ended up having to get a new one installed. It cost me $825, which believe it or not, was a deal. I am really upset about it, but I now have my beloved hot water.

The 4-year-old water heater sat defunct in my driveway draining pathetically on the lawn. I looked at it from the window as my plumber was installing the new one and advising me about the issues with purchasing water heaters from the home improvement store and that particular brand of water heater. It's funny, I thought, that no one mentions all these issues at the time. I let him drone on and glared at the sad water heater, drip, drip, drip. I cursed it and imagined myself taking a baseball bat to it. Perhaps in my younger days but I'm much too Zen for that now.

My plumber offered to take the old water heater with him but I decided I wanted to personally preside over its demise and took it to our local recycling center. You never get very much for anything you bring there, but I had no intention of paying for its removal and I do believe strongly in recycling everything I can.

As soon as my plumber left, I popped the water heater from hell in the back of the Prius and off to recycling I went. I knew recycling closes at noon on Saturdays so I had to hustle to make it on time. After some minor mishaps, I got my receipt and proceeded to the cashier's window. The cashier is this really sweet and funny blonde lady. I hadn't seen her since the beginning of the year, so we chatted a bit which the other people in line didn't appreciate, totally understandably. I turned my head to those behind me in line to smile apologetically and as I did, out of the corner of my eye, what do you think I spotted on the floor of the recycling center? Bag O' Tools! I couldn't believe it. The recycling center has a big sign that says they buy tools, but just as with their recycling rates, the amount they pay is pennies on the dollar. I told my friend behind the counter my story with the tools and what I offered. She told me that the woman should have taken the offer because they only paid $10.

Well, you could have knocked me over with a feather. Poor Bag O' Tools. It looked so sad sitting there in its dirty canvas bag amongst all the refuse of the neighborhood. I wanted to offer them the $10 for it and rescue them but they wouldn't have taken so little and the line I was in to get out of there before they closed had grown. So, I decided against discussing further and wished her well.

Imagine, that seller could have sold the tools for $60 and ended up with $10. Even if she had accepted the $47, she would have done better than $10. Sellers, please learn from this seller's mistake. Don't get stuck on the numbers. Clearly the woman did want to get rid of the tools because she gave them away for $10 instead of trying to sell them another way. If your goal is to get rid of it all, get rid of it all! If you're selling for $10 and someone offers you $5, sell it. If you're goal is to get rid of everything, that's one step closer to your goal. If you feel that you should get the $10, you might, or you might have to sell it to recycling.

SHOW ME THE MONEY SALE

I think a lot of sellers come from the perspective of thinking, "Oh, I can get rid of all this crap and make a little cash" but what they really mean is "I need some extra cash, what can I sell?" It's a mind game that we don't really realize we're playing. You look at that old computer monitor that you stored in your garage because you got a nice big 30" now. "I've got to get rid of that thing." The old monitor is just gathering dust and taking up space so it's got to go. "I could easily get $100 for that." Uh, no you can't. "But I paid $500 for it." Ugh, I cannot tell you how many times I hear, "but I paid….". Your item is only worth what the market will bear and honestly, I don't care what you paid for it, it's like a car, drive it off the lot and it's lost half its value. If you don't think you can part with your monitor for less than $100, then your motivation is to make money and not to get rid of stuff.

Don't get the impression that I condemn sales trying to make extra cash. Just be honest with yourself about your motivation and plan accordingly. There is nothing wrong with trying to make something off your items, but it means you'll have to sell in volume. Let me explain; let's say you need to make $200 for an unexpected bill. You think, "I can sell all this crap and make a boatload of money." This is where my words come in and throw cold water on that thought. You really have to go for a volume sale if you're attempting to earn a certain dollar amount. Sell a ton of stuff and keep the prices dirt cheap. You want money coming in left and right. This brings a crowd and encourages the crowd to spend. I think people see other people at a sale and all of a sudden you need a traffic officer. I've seen this happen recently:

About three weeks ago, I was driving home after a hike with my dogs and I went through the neighborhood looking for sales. There are rarely any good sales, but this day was different.

There were two sales on the same street only six houses separated them. One sale had masses of people, literally, everywhere you looked were people. The other sale had three people.

At the first sale there were people trying to find places to park and deals being done left and right. At the second sale there was a man sitting in a lawn chair listening to the radio. This is no exaggeration folks.

I sat in my car and studied both sales for a moment to study the differences and the reasons for them. The first sale was a quasi-estate sale. It was run by an outside interest, a church, the person who owned the house sadly passed away and was apparently a big fan of QVC. There was every kind of kitchen appliance known to man. Most everything was still in its original box and some things unopened. With a few exceptions, most of these items were $20 or less. There was a complete set of pots and pans in the box for $60 and I believe that was the highest price item they had.

I thoroughly enjoyed this sale. I made deals left and right. The only thing I was upset about was not getting an Instapot for $15 because its power cord was missing. In talking with one of the people running the sale, she said, "We'll probably be back next week." I laughed and told her, "No, you won't". I could tell that they would be sold out by noon at the latest. They were.

The other sale was still rather dismal. Most of the items for sale were yard/garden items. There was a small generator that had a price of $200. A ladder for $100 and a rather nice large spade shovel that was priced at $15(Yikes).

Are you starting to see a pattern? I drove past the lawn chair man's sale again the next day (Sunday) to see how he was doing. He must have gone into the house because he wasn't sitting in the lawn chair anymore. There were a few people milling around but he needn't worry about missing a sale.

Two sales six houses apart: One closed early the other couldn't sell a shovel. The difference between a successful sale and a total bomb isn't complex but there are several ways the man in the lawn chair went wrong.

- Sheer volume of items. Lawn chair man didn't have enough to fill a table, let alone his driveway. Whereas the "estate sale" was packed with items in boxes with pretty pictures on them. Enticement is exciting for customers. All these things still in their boxes makes the customer think they're getting brand new at an amazing deal.

- Prices, Prices, Prices. – We have a whole chapter on pricing in this book but here's a slight preview. Your prices have to be rational. Selling a shovel, cute as it may be, for $15 isn't rational. Expecting someone to be walking around with $200 to spend on a generator, isn't rational. The general rule is, think about what you would pay for something used at a garage sale. Consider how much cash you carry on your person at any one time. Right now, I think I have $34. I don't think $200 for the generator was a bad price per se, but I did do a check on my phone and discovered that the retail price was $269. Now $69 is a substantial discount at the store, but not at a garage sale.

The biggest difference between these two sales was MOTIVATION. At the quasi-estate sale, the motivation was clearly to move items. Lawn Chair man may have wanted to clear out the clutter, but his prices belied that notion. Let's speculate that he wanted to make $500. I base that figure on the items he had for sale and the prices he was asking for them. The higher end items did not sell, the $15 spade may have sold, because I didn't see it the next day, but doubtful at least at that price. By Sunday, he was still short of his goal by over $400.

The quasi-estate sale was sold out by noon Saturday morning. Now, I couldn't tell you how much they made, but I would guess that achieving Lawn Chair man's goal would not have been an issue. But a key difference was that quasi-estate sale wanted to move merchandise.

It can be tempting to just put a few signs out and open the garage door, but if you don't have a lot, it just isn't an appealing sale to go to and it then becomes a waste of your time. A "virtual" garage sale is a much better way to sell items like generators, large tools, anything you won't sell for pennies on the dollar. You're also more likely to be successful in selling these items than you would be at a garage sale simply because an ad for a generator targets a specific customer. Having a generator at your sale is fine, but the likelihood of the right customer stopping by your sale is a long-shot.

If you do have a lot to move, a good rule of thumb is keeping the majority of your items $20 or less. That's about the most cash people carry around with them, on average, and the general dollar amount they won't mind or question spending. Anything over that amount makes people start asking themselves, "Do I really need this?"

Here's another important tip/lesson: Check your prices online. You might think this is a pretty obvious step, but I don't think it is, or at least it doesn't seem to be. I think we're often blinded about the value of our stuff. I find when I post something for sale, I've often valued it higher than the market is willing to spend. It's only when I start looking at similar items and what they are priced at, that I realize I am over-valuing my item.

> I'm currently looking for a sofa and possibly a matching love seat. I always look for used before buying new. I could get an entire living room set for $1000, but if I can

help a neighbor by purchasing their set for $300, well that's a no-brainer. I search all the lists and have found several possibilities, but the prices are really irrational. I just reviewed a new ad posted in just the last day. It's a three-seater couch, a couple of years old, no damage. The price? $500. Just for the couch. Folks, the new one I'm looking at is $399. I'm selling my massive sectional for $200 but her three-seater is worth $500. I actually checked with her because I thought it was a mistake. It was not. Once again, the seller shared that it was only a few years old and how she spent so much for it. If there's one thing, one hope I have for this book it's to get sellers to stop telling people how much you paid for the item you now want to sell. It is ridiculously annoying and it means nothing. I'm not really sure what people are trying to get across when they tell you, "well I paid $100K..". What does that mean? Are you saying I should give you more because *you* couldn't negotiate a better deal?

Here's a quick tale from a purchase I made this week: Several years ago, I purchased a storage bench from Burlington, which is a kind of outlet store near my home. It was the perfect shade of off-white and went nicely with my furniture. I negotiated a deal with the store manager because it had some minor defects and secured the bench for $50.

As with most things in life and particularly in my home, the bench got destroyed. The dogs were puppies then and teething and chewed a hole in the base of the bench. I was not pleased, but honestly, it was getting old and I love the dogs more than my stuff, so it's gone. For several months I looked for another one. I could never find the right color. I ended up with a gray one which was really awful and cheap looking but I did need the storage, so I lived with it.

This weekend, I was checking out the online apps and low and behold, there's my bench. The exact same color and style as my old beloved off-white storage bench. I wanted to buy it right away but the seller wanted $100.

Storage benches are just ridiculously priced. Even the one I bought at Burlington. I mean, it's a BOX. They're not even well made, it's just insane. Some were nearly $200 at the outlet store. One of the reasons I ended up with the one I did was because I wouldn't spend up.

I favorited her bench because I knew the seller wouldn't get her price and the price would come down. Favorite-ing, is kind of like putting a pin in something you like and want to get back to at some point. It's a risk. Someone else could snap it up and you're out of luck. I figured it was a risk worth taking. There was no way I was going to spend $100 on a box, right color or not. If someone else got it, fine. You have to detach yourself from these items. It's not easy, but if it's right, it will be there.

As predicted, this week the price came down. I got notified of a price reduction from the app and looked and she'd only reduced the price by $10. I reached out to her. I explained that the price was just too high and what do you think she said? "Well I paid, $129 at T.J. Maxx" The smart ass in me says, "Well just because you're a sucker..." The mean girl in me says, "So the *!#* what?" The responsible, mature me replies: "I see, I can offer $50 if that's something you can do." I got the bench which is now where the old one was. The seller made a point of

showing me the price tag when I picked it up as if that
was going to make me change my mind and give her
another $50. As though I would say, "Oh my god, I have
to give you more money now that I've seen the price you
paid!"

Sellers, stop telling your sale-ers what you spent on your
stuff. It's pointless. It doesn't matter. And it's incredibly
annoying.

The "It's all Gotta Go Now!" Sale

We've discussed the "Let's make some money" sale. But
there is another kind of sale; the "clean-out" sale. These are
the sales where the people are getting rid of everything.
Their number one priority is to get it out and whatever is left
at the end of their sale is landfill. The quasi-estate sale was
almost this kind of sale and that was a big reason for its
success.

I often hear sellers saying, "Oh, they just want it for nothing".
I do understand that frustration, but when I think about it I
want to reply, "So, what?" Of course, they want it for nothing
and *you* don't want it at all so what's the problem? Typically,
these sellers are in it for the money, but profess they are
motivated by getting rid of everything. As a seller and sale-
er, I cannot emphasize enough, be honest with yourself and
know what you want to accomplish. Be clear about your
goals. If it's to make a certain amount, that's fine but don't
say that you're in it to clear it. That's very frustrating for
sale-ers and won't help you achieve your goal.

If you are ready to clear, congratulations, this is the most
popular sale for real sale-ers and the type of sale most likely
to succeed. But be ready to part with things cheap.

EVERYTHING MUST GO!

Sale-ers love these sales. They're also most likely to buy something they normally wouldn't at these types of sales. I confess, I am one of those sale-ers. I bought a Sharper Image foot massager because it was $2. Why?

These sales are the most likely to succeed because the prices are low and the energy is all about getting it sold at any price. If you are a seller, you may be thinking, "well, I just can't sell it at ANY price". My response is why not? IF you are truly wanting it gone, then it goes at whatever price you can get. If you have a flat screen and someone says I'll give you $20 for it. Announce to the crowd assembled that you just got an offer of $20 for a flat-screen tv. See what happens. Literally tell the crowd, "Hey everyone, I just got an offer of $20 for this flat screen, any better offers?" You will get swarmed with folks wanting to pay you more. Bet on it. I've seen it happen with a power-washer.

A Sale-er's Dream

Every avid garage sale-er is looking for that one sale, the sale of sales, the sale with all the cool junk at dirt cheap prices. This sale will have a huge amount of stuff. All kinds of random impedimenta from TV trays from the 1970s to table saws. All of which has one thing in common, it's all got to go!

These sales are a rare find. My neighbor Kim has garage sale selling down-pat. Once she decides it's got to go, she wants it gone and whatever she can get for it, she accepts. Her sales are definitely not to be missed. She may not always have a lot of stuff but what she has doesn't stick around long. It's not that her stuff is all that amazing but it's good practical things that are dirt cheap and never go amiss. I bought a bunch of mixing bowls from her. The good heavy ceramic ones from the 70s. I bought a pail with mop wringer. And my absolute favorite, I bought a table saw. Tools are my one weakness. Everything was dirt cheap and she sold out. Much of her merchandise sold to me.

Sale-ers, to find these sales isn't easy, but I'm not telling you something you don't already know. You will probably be kissing a lot of frogs before you find that prince of a sale. The tip I have for you sale-ers is to have a plan. Do some research. If all the sales you want to go to are in your neighborhood and within walking distance, then you can take a walk and see what you find. If, however, you have to get in your car to get to the sale of choice, try to determine what other sales are in that neighborhood so you have other options if the one you choose is a bust. Try to pick neighborhoods with a good number of sales. I like to visit community sales where a good number of families are participating. This will increase your odds of finding the great "everything must go" sale and decrease your gas and time expenditure.

Review the online ads for Garage Sales. This will help you map out a plan for your Saturday, but it also helps you locate the good sales. If you read ads on Craigs or OfferUp or Letgo, you can get an idea of the seller's motivation from the ad. It's not a guarantee. Many sellers claim they have to sell everything but it turns out they have to sell everything at a price. If you're unsure about a sale, save it for last. In fact, even the sales where the prices are too high, shouldn't be written off completely. Come back the next day, if you can. Try them before they close up shop. Having to stuff all their stuff back in the garage can be a real motivator for making a sale.

For the seller with an "everything must go" perspective, garage selling is going to be a lot more entertaining and not take up the majority of your weekend. These sales move merchandise fast. People are happy with getting a pail with a mop wringer for a dollar, even if they don't need it. Happy customers are fun! They laugh and joke with you and vice versa. If your goal is to get rid of everything regardless of cost, you'll have a very successful sale indeed.

As a seller, you might be saying, "Well I don't want to sell my cordless drill for $5. Does that mean I won't have a successful sale?" Absolutely not. What it does mean is that you'll have to seriously think about your priorities and the best way to proceed.

I have an amazing cordless drill and there's no way I would sell it period, let alone for $5. But in this case, a garage sale isn't necessarily the best place to sell it. If it's so high end, then an app or even eBay is the way to go. I have another cordless drill that has a NiCad battery. That one should be sold for $5-10, if I intended to sell it. Things have value and I would never suggest that you give your possessions away, but the garage sale is a magical place where all things are possible and dirt cheap. At least at the successful sales. There are other places where you can sell higher end items for higher profits, it's just the garage sale really isn't necessarily one of them.

Let's say you have a fantastic 20-volt Dewalt cordless impact driver and drill with batteries and charger. This set sells retail for about $200. (I got mine for $100 misprint ad @ that home improvement store I got the water heater ☺) Clearly, selling it for $10 at a garage sale would get it sold so fast your head would spin. That's not likely to happen, Sale-ers, nor is it expected of you, Sellers. But let's say you do want to sell your set and the garage sale is a perfect opportunity. Here's how you want to proceed:

1. Place all higher-end items in a section on their own. Inside the garage or closest to the home is best. They should be nearest the home for two reasons: 1) loss-prevention and 2) customers should have to go through all your other stuff to get to it. This helps them see all you have to offer. Sale-ers can get focused on one item and miss the rest of the show.

2. Make sure whatever you have that you want a price for is working, i.e. charged, plugged in, gassed up and testable. If you're going to ask for $100 for something, you should be able to demonstrate it's working condition. (another mistake Bag o' Tools lady made)

3. When you're doing your online advertising, which we'll discuss in detail in a later chapter, create a separate ad for the higher end item and reference that ad in your garage sale ad. Why? The reason you want to create a separate ad is because if the higher end item doesn't sell at the garage sale, you can leave the high-end item ad up after you've taken the garage sale ads down. This helps you in a number of ways, but most importantly, you are telling potential customers that this item will be on display at your upcoming garage sale. This puts potential customers at their ease. It's not always easy to arrange a time and place to meet and personal safety is always a concern for customers so the opportunity to view the item out of doors and in public is very appealing. It saves you from setting meeting times and missed connections. It also helps in a less visible way. If your customer knows that you're having a garage

sale and the item in question will be on display at that sale, the serious buyer will attempt to be the first to arrive at your sale in order to beat out other customers.

Higher end items can sell at garage sales, you simply need to be very clear about the prices for these items and advertise well beforehand so the Sale-ers come prepared. Remember that no one carries cash anymore, which is another good reason you keep your prices low. Do your due diligence as well. I may think my Dewalt set is worth $200, but the sold price is probably about $75. I often see tools not nearly as nice as mine and the list price is maybe $10 less than retail. That's just dumb. As a seller, you have to make it worth someone's while. Think about what you would spend to buy your item used. If an item is $100 at Walmart but you're selling yours for $90; it's hardly enough to motivate a buyer. Blow out any retailer's pricing. If Walmart sells it for $100, sell yours for $35. Make it nearly impossible for the Sale-er to walk away from your deal. The only difference between you and Walmart should be the return policy.

When you do your research, look at the sold ads and not just the currently selling ads. If finding the sold price is difficult to locate, check the more expensive ads and see how long the ad has been posted. These are real clues as to what you're likely to get for your high-end items.

The bottom-line for Sellers is to understand your motivation. If you find that you can't part with something dirt cheap, more than likely you really don't want to part with it at all. That's okay too, just understand that going in. If you find that you do want to get rid of it but the money is a concern, consider the best way to get the price you want. It may not be a garage sale. If you find yourself buried in stuff and your primary concern is getting it out of your house and not in a landfill, well then, let's get started.

Chapter 2. Get the Lingo Down

Did you know that the name of a sale can make a difference in the success of your sale? Garage Sales come in all kinds of styles and shapes and yes, names. There are Yard Sales, Moving Sales, Estate Sales, Alley Sales, the list goes on and on. But what's the difference? Many times, it's just the location and the name reflects this, but not always. Sometimes the name will give you a hint of things to come. If you are planning a sale or would like to visit one, consider the name of the sale carefully and what it says to potential customers. The name of a sale sends a message and sets expectations. This seems like a small thing, but very often it's a key indicator of success or failure. Read on.

What's in a Name:

Estate Sales

Signs for Estate sales are rather intriguing, the words Estate Sale invoke Gatsby-like images of mansions and amazing hidden treasures from the past. The reality is far less romantic. Typically, these are sales run by companies that sell whole households of items from someone who has sadly past away. These sales are frequented by antique hunters and dealers looking for a rare find and have money to spend. These sales are not cheap. The company hired takes a portion of the profits so wheeling and dealing is limited if at all.

Two personal experiences: the first estate sale I went to was in an upper-middle class neighborhood called Highland Park. I saw the sign and decided to stop. I walked up to the door, estate sales are typically held in the home, and there was a sort of bouncer-type guy at the door who announced to me that I had to take off my shoes before entering. I then saw a sign behind him that reiterated the message. The floors were covered in that sticky plastic that people put on to protect their new carpets. I suppose asking people to remove their shoes isn't the most unreasonable request, but I have some orthopedic issues and even if I didn't, I want to wear my shoes. It's weird to ask people to take them off. I, very nicely, advised bouncer dude that I had some issues and needed the support of my shoes and he said, "Well I guess you're not coming in, then are you?" Note the quote marks. This was my first encounter with Estate Sale company employees, surprisingly, it wasn't the worst.

The next (and last) estate sale I went to was in a somewhat low-end neighborhood called Prospect Heights. Another sale run by a company which clearly had issues with customer service. The home itself was just a standard bungalow. This made me think that whatever was there would be reasonably priced. I was mistaken. The prices were pretty ridiculous. $600 for a set of china that was "antique" if you consider being made in the 1950s antique. I was about to leave when I noticed a jewelry display table with three jewelry display cases and three corresponding workers behind each display. The cases were those large rectangular, felt lined cases with a glass top so you could peer at the items it contained. As I passed, a costume ring caught my eye. It's always amusing how these places try to pass off costume as something of value to raise the price. I stopped at the case for a better look. I asked the worker, a woman in her mid-50s, if I could see the ring. She took the ring out of the case and as I reached for it, she snatched her hand back. I kind of looked stunned and she noticed this and said "You can't touch it." I was completely rocked by this statement and stammered, "What?" She had the nerve to say that she didn't want anyone stealing it. Yeah, seriously. What's worse, there was a security guard not ten feet away. Folks, it was a costume ring. Quality costume, yes, but costume nonetheless. I cannot tell you how nasty this woman was and it was clear there was an element of bias that was truly disgusting. I actually complained to the owner of the company regarding the incident. Shockingly, the owner supported the worker's behavior which I suppose suggests that it was top-down. I posted a Yelp review regarding the company and the incident. The owner then sent me some rather vicious messages and I was left to wonder who would hire these people to do anything? The end result, as you might imagine, no more "estate sales".

Having said all this, I don't want to deter all you "sale-ers" out there from going on your own estate sale adventure. I'm quite certain they all can't be as bad as what I encountered or the businesses that perform these services wouldn't be successful. In addition, not all "estate sales" are run by an outside firm. Keep in mind, while this is the "typical" definition of an Estate Sale, it is by no means the only definition. Lately, some families go rogue and call their sale an Estate Sale. Why? Well it could be that they are clearing out a departed loved one's home or perhaps it's simply a way to denote the kind of customer they wish to attract. Sometimes a seller just thinks it sounds better to call their sale an estate sale. This is why I wrote this chapter. Sellers be careful of the messages you may be unintentionally sending to potential customers. Sale-ers, keep an open mind when you plan your adventure; within limits. If the sale is in your neighborhood and the only cost to you is time, then by all means, if not or you're not sure, save the estate sale for the last stop of the day. What you encounter can be amazing. Just manage your expectations carefully.

Sellers, consider carefully before crossing out "garage" and writing in "estate" on your signs. Personally, I will drive past an estate sale. Many seasoned sale-ers do not attend estate sales. Consider what you have for sale and what kind of customer you're trying to attract. You'll hear me repeating this to you sellers regularly because it is the number one issue sellers encounter. For those who regularly visit sales, it's their number one pet peeve. If the difference between a successful sale and re-packing all your crap can be measured by the way you advertise, shouldn't you consider carefully?

If you have some high-end items and you're not willing to part with them cheaply, the estate sale is a viable option. You should also consider a local auction house. We have a local auction house that does a fantastic job and doesn't charge much. The items they auction can be anything from cars to nails. I rarely buy from them because I'm not looking to pay more than everyone else for anything. But I have purchased some items and I think if you have a few high-end items but not enough for a full-blown estate sale, an auction house is a good way to go.

eBay is often an option for sellers with a few higher end items, but note that eBay is not what it once was. eBay-ers tend to buy from sellers with a reputation making it hard for the first and/or one-time seller. These sellers usually have to sell pretty low and the eBay fees are significant.

Amazon is also an option. This might surprise you, but if you notice when you're shopping on Amazon there sometimes is a little blurb asking if you have one for sale. This is your invite to sell something on Amazon. You'll go through a few steps and it may not be as easy as placing a Craigslist ad, but you will certainly get the traffic which no other site can match.

The biggest downside with these options is shipping. If you've got grandma's bedroom set from 1846, shipping it somewhere is going to be cost prohibitive and probably the last thing you want to do. So what else can you do?

THERE'S AN APP FOR THAT!

The two most popular online sale apps, as I'm writing, are Letgo and Offerup. Craigslist does not have an app but Classifieds 2.0 puts CL at your fingertips. We'll get more into these options in the advertising chapters, but these apps are terrific free-to-cheap options for items that are specialty or just don't fit in the "garage-sale" price range.

So, are we anti-estate sale? No, not really, these sales serve a purpose, but it's good to be savvy about the messages you're sending to potential customers. Additionally, if you're a sale-er, know before you go. Estate Sale does not say all are welcome or I need everything gone. It says, "I need everything gone at a price". If that works for you, then by all means, Estate Sale it.

THE YARD SALE

Yard sales are typically sales at apartment or multi-family dwellings without a garage. But not always. In naming sales, we can be a bit haphazard and that can cost you sales. You think, "well, I'm putting all the stuff in the yard so I'll call it a Yard Sale". That's perfectly reasonable but to seasoned sale-ers Yard sale says; just some household items, pots and pans, toys, knick-knacks. This is perfectly fine if that's what you have on offer. If you want to sell a couch, however, or perhaps quilts or comforters, calling it a yard sale may hurt you. Yard sale denotes items you don't mind having on your lawn. Your old couch or the quilt your grandmother made may or may not be something you'd want to put in the yard. Still, if all you have to display your couch is your yard, then it's just a name, but you'll want to be clear about what you have on offer. If you have larger or just items not commonly expected at a yard sale, be sure your audience knows it.

Sale-er, it's easy to dismiss the Yard sale. When you see a yard sale you may think it small and not having much but just as I want Sellers to be careful about how they name their sale, we Sale-ers need to be wise about how we judge a sale worthy of our time and interest. We'll discuss how to plan your g-sale adventure in-depth in later chapters, but I would suggest here that for those sales you aren't sure about, make a note of their location and perhaps do a drive-by to ascertain interest. There are so many times I've dismissed a sale I thought didn't have anything only to discover that it was the best sale of the year. Still other times I've been just certain of a sale and it turns out to be a bust. Some sales I've literally wanted to scratch out garage sale and change their signs to read, "NOTHING BUT GARBAGE AT TERRIBLE PRICES". Sometimes it will be hit or miss, there's really no getting around that fact, but you can be pleasantly surprised so be sure to factor some time in your hunt for the "maybe" sales.

MOVING SALES

I cannot tell you how many times I've been to moving sales that have a sofa and then a bunch of cookbooks. It's imperative that your sale name reflect the sale itself. You may be moving and want to sell the couch rather than move it to the new location, but that does not mean you're having a moving sale, you're just selling your couch. Moving sales typically are defined by customers walking into the residence and items on offer are in place in the home. In this way it's very similar to the Estate Sale, but that's where the similarity ends. The items for sale are not typically antique but there may be an antique or two. The items are priced to move. Items such as kitchenware (i.e. dishes, pots and pans, utensils), furniture (i.e. sofas, bookshelves, coffee tables, beds (note: no mattresses- more later), appliances (i.e. refrigerators, washer/dryer, dishwasher) are all items expected when customers come to a moving sale. Smaller items can also be sold at these events but are not the main event.

If you are moving and want to reduce the amount of furniture items you're taking with you, then the moving sale is the way to go. Note that customers expect the prices to be dirt cheap. Sellers, do not take it personally. We'll discuss pricing in depth later in the book, but what I want to get across to you here is that the name Moving Sale says to customers that you need to get rid of this stuff and you will do so by any means necessary. Therefore, Sale-ers are going to come at you with below sticker price offers. It is not a comment on your tastes, a reflection of the item's quality or condition, nor does it necessarily reflect their feelings on the value. Sale-ers are looking for the best possible deal full-stop. If it annoys you that the offers are too low, take a break and refocus your energy. Remember your goal; get rid of all the crap. Be careful not to dismiss low offers out of hand as you may not get another. When you get a "ridiculous" offer, pause, smile and counter. What will you accept? If an item is priced at $20 and someone offers $5, several scenarios may be happening. First, and I think the most likely, the Sale-er may not have $20. Typically, Sale-ers are low to middle income. Consider that this might be all they can afford. Second, you may have priced incorrectly. This is easily done. We'll get more into the pricing of items later, but in the end, your item is only worth what the market will bear. The point is, "low-ball" offers are not an insult but an opportunity, be careful how you react.

For Sale-ers, if you're interested in finding furniture at a drastically reduced rate, the moving sale is a spectacular place to start. However, it's important to be sure the sale is actually a moving sale and not a sofa sale. To do this, try to reach out to the seller beforehand, if possible. If this isn't possible, take clues from the advertisement. Typically, a proper moving sale has a the very least a bulleted list of items on offer. If it doesn't, chances are there isn't much to recommend it and might be a waste of time. Having said that, how many of us are organized enough to list out our items for sale when we're not moving, so this tip shouldn't be a deal-breaker. Consider carefully and plan accordingly. If a side trip to a sale you're not sure of won't break the bank or send your schedule into a black hole, then check it out. If it's nothing, at the very least you won't be wondering and if it's an amazing sale, you won't be kicking yourself for not checking it out.

Typically for moving sales, there is a lot of advertisement. Most likely Craigslist is the seller's first choice. This is because unlike a garage sale, the moving sales are typically contained in the home itself and so the seller cannot rely on drive-by traffic. Advertising is so important, whatever sale you have, but for the real moving sale it's critical. As a sale-er, reliance on the advertising is inevitable. It's not that I won't stop for one if I'm driving by, but if I'm looking for furniture or household items, I will first look to Craigslist, then Offer-up and finally Letgo. This saves a lot of time and energy.

The Multi-Family Sale

Well this sounds promising doesn't it? Not in my neighborhood. A multi-family garage sale implies that there are multiple families selling their stuff. In my neighborhood, multi means two houses with two tables of Christmas ornaments.

The Multi-Family sale can be a real smart move. If you really don't have a lot or you have a good deal of stuff but would really like to combine resources with your friends to make the day more enjoyable, a multi-fam can be a really good idea. Sale-ers love these sales. Tons of stuff in one destination. Sellers, just be sure there is truth in your advertising. If you want to call it a multi-family sale, have:

- At least three households participating
- Tons of stuff
- Multiple locations ok if on the same street

If the location of your multi-family sale is at more than one house, all the participating houses should be in close proximity of each other. If the sales are in several places throughout the neighborhood, this is a neighborhood sale and not a multi-family sale. It's important that you accurately advertise the type of sale you're having. No one likes their time wasted, sale-ers least of all. This will directly affect the success of your sale.

THE NEIGHBORHOOD SALE

This is a particular favorite of mine. The gated community in our neighborhood has a neighborhood sale twice a year. It's rather hit or miss. Neighborhood sales can be misleading. That gated community has a ton of homes and people. They have their own park and soccer field. You'd think it would be teeming with sellers, but that is not the case. In fairness, if everyone decided to participate it might be quite the mess. It's a vast complex and I don't see how you could make it everyone, but I'd sure like to try.

The problem is getting everyone to participate. It's a lot to ask. You'll never get everyone. Things happen and emergencies come up or it's just not the best weekend for them. The problem for Sale-ers is neighborhood sales are so hit or miss. There might be one sale or ninety. One street will have three sales but the street you're on doesn't have any. Do you keep searching or do you move on to a sure thing? When you get a good neighborhood sale, it's fantastic. The community I mentioned had one two years ago with some amazing things. This year was pretty dismal.

Would you like to organize a neighborhood sale? If you can get your neighborhood to participate, the neighborhood sale can be a real treat. It takes someone with great organizational skills to make it happen. If it's something you'd like to try, I've devoted a bonus chapter on how to organize a neighborhood sale at the end of the book.

THE GARAGE SALE

A great garage sale is a thing of beauty. Is that overstating it?
I don't think so. When I find a great sale, my heart just soars.
I'm not a big fan of shopping, but I do love to save money. I
love to meet my neighbors and strike a deal. Doesn't really
matter what the object is or isn't. If it can be used and is a
good deal, then I am jubilant.

I once furnished an entire apartment from one garage sale. It
was an apartment I had in Arlington Heights. I got a dining
room table and chairs, pictures for the wall, dishes and
dozens of other things all needed as I was coming from a
much smaller space and some things were sold in my own
sale prior to the move. That garage sale has stayed with me
all these years because it was perfect. Everything I needed,
all in one spot. Rock-bottom pricing. They weren't precious
or expensive items. Just everyday use stuff at dirt cheap
prices. I'm not a person that would spend thousands on
furniture. I do appreciate it when I see it, but I'm perfectly
fine with nice looking, good condition, lower-end items.

So, what makes a great garage sale? Well, first and foremost
is the items for sale, second is the price. We're going to
discuss in detail what and what not to sell, but just for this
segment, let's keep it simple and say that the idea of a garage
sale is to sell the items you would normally store in your
garage. This isn't a strict rule or anything, I'm only referring
to what the name "Garage Sale" implies. Garage sale sounds
like; bikes, tools, toys, lawn mowers, maybe some furniture,
etc. These are the kinds of things I believe I will find. So,
when I go to a "Garage Sale" and I find all the clothes from
your closet in your driveway on racks like J.C. Penney, suffice
it to say, I'm disappointed. Welcome to my neighborhood.

Last Friday, I was driving home and about two blocks from the house I saw a garage open and racks upon racks of clothes. I'll go on a proper rant about this later, but that is not a garage sale. This is a constant issue in my neighborhood and one I don't think will resolve itself anytime soon. Despite these sales doing little to no business, they are out there every weekend until the snow starts to fly.

Generally, your sale should have cool stuff at cheap prices. The cool stuff is open somewhat to interpretation but it should be things you would expect or at least advertised differently. If the sale in my neighborhood stated, "clothing sale" instead of garage sale, I would have no issue with it. I wouldn't visit it, but that's good since I don't buy used clothes and am not the audience for that sale.

When you are clear about the items you are selling, you will get the desired audience and you won't get someone like me who is now annoyed that you wasted their time.

THE "YOUR NAME HERE"-SALE

I once saw an ad for a sale called: "Grandma's Attic" sale. It was just what you would think was in Grandma's attic. Toys, Christmas ornaments, clothes, crafting material, etc. This is what you would expect and the name reflected what was on offer. That is the key. The name of your sale sends a message to the audience of what you are offering, therefore choose carefully. Whether you choose to call it a Garage sale, Yard sale, Car boot sale, Estate sale, or stuff from my school locker sale, be sure that the name of the sale reflects what you have to offer. This seems like a small matter when considering the larger picture, but as I've tried to demonstrate, the name of a sale can speak directly to the customer you'd like to attract. So, if you don't have a garage or the items you have to sell are not what one would think of when you think of a garage sale, consider tailoring the name of the sale to the kind of things you're selling. If that seems strange, consider these ads I found on Craigslist under "Garage Sale":

Jewelry Sale – Handcrafted and Designer Jewelry

Car Parts Garage Sale

Massive Antiques and Collectibles Sale

Barnyard Sale – Farm tools and sports equipment

Samples Sale – Designer Bags and Luggage

Holiday Décor Sale

Whatever you have to sell, chances are there's a buyer, if you can find them. There's no point in reaching out to an expectant mother in search of baby items if you have a garage full of tools. Don't waste your time or that of your customer. Be selective and clear on what you have and know your audience, which incidentally is what we talk about in our next chapter.

Chapter 3. Know Your Audience

Garage Sale-ers come from every walk of life. They come in every size, shape and color. The one thing they all have in common is the desire for a great deal. Some are savvier than others, but all know a deal when they see one. If you want to sell, knowing what you have, who will want it and how to let them know are the keys to having a successful sale.

For Sale-ers the task of finding your seller can be just as frustrating. The key to finding that amazing deal is largely out of your hands in many ways. If the seller hasn't advertised properly or doesn't clearly communicate what they have, the deal is lost. I've had many a frustrating experience just missing out on a deal because the information wasn't communicated.

What do I have for Sale

Sellers: Any successful sale is going to require a bit of due diligence on your part. Consider what you want to get rid of. Whether it's an entire storage locker or just the extra boxes of "stuff" you have in the attic, review it all carefully. It's best to make an inventory of the items. If you don't know what you have, it's very difficult to determine a buyer. Once you know what you have, you'll ask yourself; "Who's looking for this?" Then we can determine the best way to communicate to your Sale-er.

An inventory of our items is our step one, step two is reviewing these items with a critical eye. We'll discuss this more in later chapters, but it's very important that you take out the memories and the emotions items have when you decide to part with them. If you cannot bear to part with that lamp for anything less than $100 because your grandmother

gave it to you and you miss her terribly. Keep the lamp. No
one is going to pay $100 for a garage sale lamp no matter
how valuable you think it is. A Tiffany lamp would have
trouble getting $100 because a garage sale is not the place to
sell a Tiffany lamp. This is what knowing your audience is all
about. There are places to sell certain items. We'll dig
deeper into what to and what not to sell at a garage sale, but
for now consider that something of such high value probably
isn't something that should be sold at a garage sale. IF it is so
valuable, consider another sale platform, like eBay, Craigslist,
Offerup or an auctioneer.

I would never tell you that your stuff isn't worth what you
think it is, but I will tell you that your perspective with
regards to the value of your items is skewed. Any item is
only worth what the market will bear. Sometimes the reality
of that fact hits us square in the face at the most inconvenient
of times.

Let's get started:

1. Gather ALL the items you want to get rid of (notice I
   did not say all the items you want to SELL)
2. Inventory these items. List what they are, their
   condition and what you THINK its value is
3. Based on your inventory, determine what kind of sale
   should you have
4. Based on your inventory, who's your buyer? Who is
   out there right now looking for the stuff you have?

GATHERING EVERYTHING YOU WANT OUT!

Before you can do your inventory, you need to have
something to inventory. Pick a spot in the living room, the

garage or maybe even your backyard and just start a pile. Anything and everything goes in the pile. If you do use the backyard, place a tarp down and pick a day with good weather, but get that pile started. Kids are a great help with this kind of project.

INVENTORY YOUR ITEMS

Your inventory is going to be your best friend in achieving your goal of clearing out the junk. It may seem a pretty anal task. Why can't you just put everything out and sell? That's certainly a reasonable question. Personally, I'm not much of a planner; however, I've found that a great deal more success comes from a little extra effort when it comes to preparation.

The benefits to a carefully prepared inventory extend beyond the sale itself. I had a pair of earrings once that while they certainly weren't precious, they were a particular shade of blue that was quite striking. I had a particular outfit that I wanted to wear these earrings with but for the life of me I couldn't find them. Just by chance I found an old notebook with my inventory for a yard sale I had when I lived in an apartment in Arlington Heights. What do you think was on the inventory? I must have looked for those earrings for days. If for no other reason, an inventory will help keep you from losing your mind.

You can construct your inventory as you like, of course. I recommend you include:

- Type of item/category i.e. small appliance, tools, furniture, etc.
- Name of item

- Age of item – this is entirely optional but it does help you determine value particularly with antiques
- Item condition – again speaks to value
- Price – have a column for the price but refrain from entering prices until the inventory is complete.

Here's an example inventory:

Home Contents Inventory List

Room/area	Item/description	Age/condition	Estimated current value	Notes

I basically modified an inventory you would use for insurance valuations. Create yours as you see fit. There are several templates out there but honestly, a pad of paper, ruler and a pencil will help you achieve the result.

Be brutally honest about what you have. It can help to have a good friend at this point. You want an honest assessment. A good friend will tell you the truth. It can be very difficult to look at something you've had for years and realize it's probably only loved by you. It's like the leg lamp from "A Christmas Story", its beauty is truly in the eye of the beholder. We all have a few leg lamps around the house which is why it's important to have a friend assess your items with you. Remember not to take any assessment or criticism personally. It's all just stuff. It's the memories you keep, the rest is just junk.

WHO'S GOING TO BUY MY STUFF?

Now that you have an idea of the items you want to sell, ask yourself, "Is there a theme here?" This is a very good question because when you want to get the word out, it would help if you have something that can tie it all together. That way you can target a specific audience. For example; your daughter has turned 13 and she can't possibly have a little girl room anymore. Canopy bed (no mattresses), Disney princess dresser, chest and desk all must go not to mention all the Barbie, Bratz and Disney Princess toys. Hmmm, I'm sensing a theme here.

Clearly, we're looking for a buyer with young girls. Probably a mom or dad on a budget. While we'll dive deeper into the advertising options later on, we can still muse about what the ad should look like:

Little Princess Garage Sale – Saturday & Sunday

Entire Disney Princess Bedroom Set for sale – includes CANOPY Bed, dressers and a desk. Toy box full of toys included at no extra cost. Servants of her royal highness will also have other items from the royal household for sale at bargain prices.

A little humor always helps an ad be memorable and if they're smiling, you're halfway to the sale. Once you have your ad, consider where your audience will be most likely to see it. Obviously digital advertising on classified sites is going to be your first stop. CraigsList is the most logical place to post, but also think outside the usual. Where would a parent of young girls be? Wherever they are, your ad should be. Consider, churches, schools, kid-friendly restaurants are all good places to get the word out and very likely to help if you ask.

Including the price is usually a good idea with an ad like this. If you don't include it, people may ask or they may think it will cost too much and not ask. We'll tackle pricing in depth in the next chapter, but again, think about getting rid of the items. If you can't part with it, don't, but if you can, price it to MOVE.

WHAT IF I DON'T HAVE A THEME?

What if you review your inventory and discover that the only thing they have in common is that the items are in your house? A theme isn't critical to your sale, but it does help you target an audience which is critical. If you can't tie things together into a central theme, consider what your "star attractions" will be. What are the really cool items that are going to get attention? Tools? Electronics? Art Supplies? Baby stuff?

These "star" items are a clue to your audience. If it's something like tools, you would be targeting, homeowners, contractors and hobbyists. You may not have enough to make it a "Theme", but in your advertising you will need to call attention to these items. It can be difficult to determine your "star" items. With furniture or appliances, you have that wow factor. Smaller items don't draw the eye the way a Bike would. Generally, the higher end items, luxury items, things that most people classify as "nice to have" but don't splurge on due to the expense. But if they can get it at bargain prices....

Whatever you have to sell, there is an audience for it. Car lovers, tool lovers, book lovers, art lovers, foodies, geeks, sci-fi fans, the list goes on forever. There's something you have that they want. Review your inventory. Ask yourself the same question for every item on your list. Who is this for? Who's been looking for this? I find it helpful to add a column to the inventory listing the audience for each item. If you find a particular audience for the majority of the items on your inventory, congratulations you've found your theme.

CHAPTER 4. PRICING THE PRICELESS

*Warning, this chapter may make you want to chuck the whole book. *

Now that's a clever way to start a chapter, isn't it?

I've referred to this section in my notes as the "tough love" section because it won't be easy to hear. However, if you read through and test the theory and do the practice exercises, I think you'll find that this is the one chapter you won't be able to do without.

Pricing your stuff for sale comes with some pitfalls that you don't see until it's too late. Have you ever had a sale and someone came up to you with one of your items and said, "How much is this?" you tell them how much it is and they promptly place it back where it came from? Or how about this, you have something marked $10, a customer comes up and offers you $2? What did you say to them at that moment? "Get lost," "no way," or "Okay, sure thank you." I'm thinking the "Okay sure" didn't happen and thank you certainly didn't. If you did accept the offer, good for you. $2 is less than $10 but more than nothing. Nothing sucks. Nothing means it's still in your house like the skunk smell after your dog got sprayed.

The first chapter of this book is about motivation for a reason. You'll have to take real stock of what you want to accomplish and not get hung up in what you think you should get for any one item. Before you even think about having a garage sale, you'll have to fully detach yourself from your stuff. It doesn't matter what you paid for it. It doesn't.   If price is truly a concern, do not have a garage sale. Sell your items on one of the many platforms available to you. You probably still won't get what you think it's worth, but you'll have a better shot than at a garage sale. Because a good and profitable garage sale is about moving merchandise. No, I'm not saying you give it away for free, but if you turn away a sale because they didn't offer you a price you think your item should fetch, you're on a path to putting all your stuff back in your garage or indeed giving it all away to Goodwill.

Here's something for you to consider, that sale I mentioned earlier, the quasi-estate sale, I asked some of the people there how they found out about the sale. I personally only saw a sign on the corner. I thought the answer I would get was that an announcement was made at their church as the sale was run by church volunteers. Instead, I was told more often than not, that they heard about it from someone who was at the sale earlier. I must have asked half a dozen people and they all said, so and so told me about it. I found that particularly interesting. Word-of-mouth is still a powerful selling tool. When you're considering offers on your items, consider the larger picture. While the offer may be less than you wanted, the larger picture is that accepting the offer will make this customer happy. This customer has helped you get rid of your junk. This customer is going to tell her neighbor of the great deal she got at your garage sale. Neighbor comes to check out the sale and get her own great deal at your garage sale. You get rid of more junk.

I am not suggesting that you take whatever anyone offers you. I am suggesting that you listen to the offer with an open mind. I am suggesting that you think about the larger picture of getting rid of the stuff you don't want. If an offer is not acceptable, take a pause and ask yourself why it's not acceptable. Why are you tempted to reject the offer? What are your reasons? If it's because you spent $$$ on it, that's a lousy answer. If it's' because you think it should fetch $$$, that's a lousy answer. If you think you can get more from the sale-er, counter.   This is really the only acceptable reason and reaction to a low offer. You can just reject it out of hand. I did have a situation once where a neighbor tried to scam me on an item I had for sale. My spidey-sense told me he was bogus and sure enough he was. That's the kind of thing you just have to reject and not what I'm referring to when I suggest you consider every offer carefully. I want you to ask yourself if it's worth it to reject a legit offer. I want you to examine your reasons before you reject the offer out of hand. Finally, I want you to consider the bigger picture and potential outcomes of your decision.

It seems a lot for just rejecting a silly offer. But if the difference between a successful sale and an utter disaster is determined by a decision you made to reject a low offer, perhaps a little careful consideration is warranted. If you reject an offer and an hour later you see the traffic to your sale has diminished, you might ask yourself if that rejection caused the sudden drop. It's unlikely, but you don't know who is nearby and overhears or is turned off by an interaction and that feeling spreads throughout a neighborhood. It's not overstating it when I say the energy that you bring will spread with every interaction. If it's one of rejection, you'll tend to get that back. If it's one of welcoming and fun, you'll get that back.

Sellers, be prepared to let stuff go. If you cannot, do not have a garage sale or at the very least don't put out items you're not willing to part with, cheap.

PERSONAL VALUE VS. ACTUAL VALUE

My mother had a very nice piano, or at least I thought it was. It was an upright. She didn't think it was nice and maybe it wasn't, I'm not an expert on pianos but it was in our home growing up and we were its third home, so it had some age and still looked pretty good. I thought it would fetch a really good price. It was a real wood Piano from the 19th century. When my mother finally sold it, she couldn't get $100 for it.

The stories that piano could have told and in the end, it wasn't worth $100. Well, there were several issues that went into its valuation. It was not the highest quality, which is going to affect anything you buy/sell. It was old tech. Shockingly, there is not a big market for antique upright pianos. We watch Antiques Roadshow and think, ooooh that rug is just like the one on the show, it must be worth $100K. It doesn't work like that. Most people showing up to the Roadshow are, in a word, disappointed. In the end, despite your item being a million years old, if the market isn't there, it just isn't worth very much. With the upright, it was old, heavy, had to be tuned a minimum of twice a year, which is very expensive. Now we carry around pianos just like guitars. It's a different age and there's no getting around that. But still, I do think there was a buyer for the piano and it was just a matter of finding the right fit. But, no matter what, there was no way it could command the amount I thought it worth. And that, in a nutshell, is my point; I see the memories, the years, the piano's story and I base it's value on its history. That's never going to work.

Everyone has a "piano" in their family and when it comes time for that item to transition to a new life with someone else, the biggest issue for you as a seller is how to take the personal value factor out of your decision making when pricing it.

I've already given you some tools to use with regards to pricing, lets expand on these tools:

1. Ask a friend to give their opinion.

    This is a great way to get honest feedback…. if you accept it. If you're going to ask a friend to help you price, have very strict rules for yourself. Your friend isn't going to want to hurt your feelings, so it's really important that first, you take your feelings out of it. Second, you make it perfectly clear to your friend that you have taken your feelings out of it.

    Whatever your friend says the price is, that's what it is, no arguments. If you disagree, that's just too bad. If you can't do it, take the item off the table and out of the sale.

    Asking a friend for help and really turning over your possessions for their assessment, is going to be really tough. You'll find out exactly how invested you are in these items. You may think your motivation is to get rid of everything. This is where you find out how true that is.

2. Research – This is kind of a no-brainer, but look at the items sold online. Check the all-powerful Google first. Google shopping will check all kinds of sites for your item and this will limit the number of places you have to check. Next be sure to search Offerup first, then Letgo second. Why that order? Offerup has a better search engine than Letgo. I recently asked Letgo for an air fryer and it showed me all kinds of things, none of which was an air fryer. Letgo just takes a bit more effort. The other advantage to

Offerup is that it shows sold listings* along with your search results. So, if you're looking to sell your air fryer, search it and the sold listing will appear with the available listings. This way you can see what the sold listings were asking for the air fryer.

*One key watch out with this method is that just because the air fryer which sold was listed at $200, doesn't mean it actually sold for $200. Offerup, takes offers on items. If the seller decides to take $50 for the air fryer you won't know.

eBay is another area which shows sold listings. This site shows the actual sold price. This is a good place to see trending sale prices. eBay isn't what it once was, so take the information with a grain of salt.

Craigslist is another site that has lost some of its luster. They've now started charging for certain ads which lost them a lot of fans. It's a bit too late to monetize the CL, but more power to them. You can't see what items have sold on the CL but you can find out what people are asking for items. The warning here is that the prices will run the gambit. While you don't see sold listings, you can surmise what might be priced poorly by the length of time the listing lasts on Craigslist. This will give you an idea of what might be a more realistic price.

3. Ask yourself what you would pay for this at a garage sale. This is a difficult assignment for some of you. You will have to disengage from the item entirely. You will have to pretend that you are seeing this item, which you bought, for the first time. It's used,

well loved, in fair to good condition. How much
would you pay?

I think this is the hardest tip to master, but it's not
impossible. The difficulty is you bought it once and in
theory you'd buy it again, but will anyone else?

4. Finally, whatever price you think something should
    be sold at, cut it in half.

    Clearly, you'll have to use reason with this tip; if
    you're selling something for a $.25, your Sale-er isn't
    going to ask for a discount and it would be difficult to
    price something at twelve and a half cents. But I do
    want you to be brutal with pricing. Take your
    emotions out of the item and then it is just stuff
    taking up space in your life. It served its purpose and
    now it's time to move on. Keep the memories, sell the
    crap.

PRICING EXERCISE

This is a practice exercise to get you ready to begin pricing
your items. You can use your phone to complete the
exercise. It's easier than it looks. The first is my example.
The first column is the item to be sold. It's an air fryer. Next,
I checked the prices on the various sites; Google, eBay,
Craigs, etc. Finally, I list my price based on what I found. The
lowest price I found what $25. I cut my price down to $15.
Now it's your turn. Complete the second line with an item of
your own. Remember to check sold listings as well as
current listings:

Item	Google lowest $	eBay lowest $	Craigslist lowest $	Offerup/Letgo lowest $	My price
Air fryer	$42.98	$25.69	$30.00	$40.00	$15
Your Item					

That probably was easier than you thought, right? It's not difficult, but it can be rather time-consuming. You couldn't be blamed for thinking, "I don't have that kind of time." My only response to you is to imagine the time you'll waste sitting at a garage sale with no customers or worse, customers and not selling anything. Any successful sale is going to require preparation on your part. Take your time, plan carefully. This exercise really doesn't take a lot of time once you've begun. Certain items that you have in bulk, items for kids like toys, costume jewelry, these are all items that can be priced at a flat rate.

I've included a template for pricing your items, just as we've done here. You can also create your own template. The point of this exercise is to emphasize the need for research. It will also help you get your head around the idea of what your items are really worth. Do you want to sell the item or do you want a price?

Let's talk about the air fryer in my example. I just bought an air fryer on a recommendation from a friend. As you now know, I don't pay full price and I'd rather give my money to a person rather than a corporation, so I found a new in box one on Offerup. She wanted $50. I paid $40. Lowest price retail was $89. Lowest price on Amazon was $129.

Turns out air fryers make terrible French fries, so I'm selling it. (I'm not selling, actually but they do make terrible fries) I have a few options, I could repost it on Offerup, Letgo, etc. Maybe even get more than I paid for it. Or I could just sell it at my garage sale. Or I could do both; post it and have it at the garage sale.

On the exercise sheet, I've listed my selling price as $15. That would mean a $25 loss for me since I paid $40. This would naturally bother me. I've used it once and I lose $25? However, if I want it gone, am I willing to take that loss and perhaps make it up on the other items in my sale? When you're faced with a decision like this, it's best to look at the whole picture and determine how to proceed. Clearly $15 for an item that sells retail $89 will make it go fast. I want it to go fast, but I also want to mitigate my losses. The strategy I come up with is this:

Re-Post the Air Fryer for $60 (leaving room for offers) on OfferUp, Letgo, and Craigs one-two weeks prior to the garage sale.

Offer it at the garage sale for $20 (leaving room for negotiation)

This strategy covers all my bases; I have it posted and if it doesn't sell, I'll have it at my garage sale. I might get the $60 or I might get $20. Either way, I'm okay with it selling at whatever price I can get and other items at the sale will help to mitigate any loss I suffer on the air fryer.

The idea with higher end items isn't about giving it away, but you'll have to look at it in terms of the bigger picture. You may not get the price you want for the item, but 1) it's out of your house, 2) you did manage to get something for it, and 3) you can balance what "loss" you suffer on one item with the sale of other items in your sale. Oftentimes, this will happen with the same buyer.

I had a G-sale a few years ago where I had a portable air conditioner as my "high-end" item. It was nice and it cooled the entire house, it was just a pain to deal with the condensation. A neighbor came by and was very interested in it. The price I put on it was $125. I gave room for negotiation and anticipated it selling at $100. My neighbor stated he wanted to buy it, but he couldn't do $125.

At this point, when you have a buyer interested but they're trying to feel you out on the price to see if they can talk you down, it's very important that you remain friendly but silent. What I mean is, keep a sort of friendly poker face. Smile as if receptive to what they're saying but no more than that. They're trying to get the lowest price they can. You would too, so there's no need to cop a 'tude. But you don't have to make it easy for them either. This is part of the fun of Selling/Sale-ing.

My neighbor talked about he was struggling and they needed this or that. I listened and politely nodded my head, but still silent. This isn't about whether he's telling the truth or not. I always assume there's some truth to a sob story. It's also not about compassion. I can show compassion for him but I'm not giving him an air conditioner. No this is just his wind-up to the pitch, he's building up to an offer. You have to know that Sellers. Don't get into a conversation, just let the Sale-er speak. The item is already sold, your pitch is over, now it's their turn.

He finally gives me a number. It's not one I like. He asks, "Will you take $75?" Hmmmm, that's a low offer. The

cheapest portable air conditioner is $250 new and this was
not the cheapest. I counter with $100. It's important to
counter, Sellers. Sale-ers want the best deal and you want
the most from your item. In the end, you do want to get rid of
the stuff so of course, use your best judgement. Still if you
can get that extra couple of dollars by countering, shouldn't
you?

My neighbor then began another mini-rant on how hot it was
and how broke he was. It was another pitch, so I waited to
see which way it would go, like an experienced catcher with a
rookie pitcher. Sorry if my sport metaphors are a little lame.
My baseball references are limited to Bull Durham and A
League of their Own.

He finally stated he didn't have more than the $75. Now I
have a dilemma. Here is someone with cash-in-hand. It's a
lot less than I was hoping for and there's a lot of interest in
this air conditioner. In fact, Sellers, air conditioners are very
popular at garage sales. But with all the interest, this person
is the only one with cash and an offer. Should I wait and see
if the other interested parties come with the full price?
Should I just take the cash he has and move the item? Should
I believe him at all?

First, it's not about the story they tell you. It could be all
bullshit and he may have $1000 in his pocket for all you
know. It doesn't matter. I think we worry a lot about losing
in a scenario like this. I think we equate taking a lesser
amount with losing out on something. It is totally
subconscious of course, but I think this is what's behind it,
you begin to think, "what if someone comes in an hour and
pays full price". This is a mind trap, it is a hope, not reality.
The reality is there is a buyer right in front of you with cash
in hand. Less than you wanted, yes, but more than you have

right now. More importantly, they are willing to pay you to take *your* junk off *your* hands. That's the reality, the rest is just nonsense.

I could have done as bag o' tools lady did and turned him away. Would I have had a similar fate? I don't know, but it was not a chance I was willing to take. I accepted the offer and he walked away happy and I made $75.

Recall I wrote earlier that every transaction should have two happy parties in order to have a successful sale. I didn't mention who should be happier. Naturally, I would have been happier with the full price. But does it follow that I was unhappy with the negotiated price? Both my Sale-er and I were very happy. My motivation was to get rid of the item, his motivation was to get it cheap. Truth be told, I only paid $75 for it myself, so I wasn't out any money even after two years of owning it. I had nothing to be unhappy about.

OH, THAT'S TOO LOW

Surprisingly, you can go too low on your prices. I doubt you'll really have this issue, but try to think like a Sale-er. If I find a 40-inch flat screen tv at a garage sale and I see the tag reads $25, chances are there's something wrong with it. You want to price according to the value of the item and adjust it for the market you are in.

Let's take the example of the flat screen. It's a couple of years old. You upgraded to a bigger one in the living room. You really don't need it in another room so you place it for sale in your garage sale. This is smart. It's the perfect thing to have at a sale. It draws a great deal of attention and it's one of those "gadgets" that people cannot resist. Also, for a struggling family, this is a real opportunity to get something they may never have been able to afford.

So, what do you price it at?

First, you do your research and check the prices online. Now since this model is a few years old, you may not be able to find a retail price for it, so CL and the online apps are your best bet to find comparable prices. Looking in my area, Chicago, I found lots of them for sale. All of them were smart TVs so for the purposes of this experiment, we'll say ours is as well. Checking Offerup, I found the highest price at $280 (which is silly) and the lowest price $100. What should our price be? If you want to move it quick, sell it for $50. This is a great price and worth the risk. If you want a bit more money, sell it for $75. Right now, you're saying, "Well of course I want more money, why wouldn't I want more money?" Because, quite simply, it's going to take longer to sell and you might not sell it at all. At $50 a Sale-er says, "What the heck?" At $75 the Sale-er says, "Well, maybe." "Well maybe" isn't good if you want it to move. It's still a good price and someone will buy it. It just might take a while longer.

A Sale-er's always weighing risk. We all weigh risk when it comes to buying something. Especially higher-end items. What if you buy this TV and it get it home and it burns out after a week? Your Sale-er doesn't know you. Even in the best of circumstances, things can go wrong. You might have sold them a TV that never gave you a moments issue and they get it home, plug it in and it starts smoking. That's the risk your Sale-er is weighing. That's why prices have to be low.

The fifty-dollar price tag gets it sold. It's an acceptable risk. Additionally, recall that I mentioned you must consider how much cash a person has on them. You want to keep these prices low because you want to complete the sale. If your Sale-er has to go to the ATM to get cash to buy your item, you've just given them extra time to reconsider. You may not see them again, so make the deal! If you're in a situation where the Sale-er simply has to go to the ATM, ask them to leave a deposit for the item. Tell them that you want to hold it for them but they'll need to put something on it. This way you know they are serious and will come back. If they say no, don't waste any more time. They aren't interested.

Sale-ers, if you are serious about an item at a sale and you're running low on cash, don't be afraid to ask for the time to get the money. I've seen many a Sale-er, short on cash but needing something, work out an arrangement on the item. Struggling families often have to float a purchase until the next paycheck. Sellers, motivated to move merchandise, are a lot more sympathetic than a payday loan.

PRICING STRATEGIES

Once you have an idea on the pricing of your items, it's important to consider your strategy for getting as close to the sticker price as you can. The strategy you use, will depend, like everything else, on your motivation. If you are motivated to get rid of everything, you will choose a strategy that fits your model. If you are motivated to get the most money for your items, you will choose a strategy that fits that model. There's no right or wrong answer and you should feel free to adopt more than one strategy as your circumstances evolve or change.

I've been to several sales over the last few years where there were no price tags on the items for sale. This is a strategy the seller was using to get the potential customer talking and also to adjust the pricing of the items to the individual customer.

There are a few advantages to this strategy. First, talking to every customer you can is a must for a successful sale. You're much more likely to sell your items when you've had good interactions with potential customers. Every attempt should be made to, at minimum, greet every customer. Without price tags, the customer is forced to communicate with seller, which gives the seller the opportunity to strike up a conversation and hopefully a sale.

Second, the seller is able to adjust pricing as necessary. When all the merchandise is tagged with a price, it becomes rather difficult for the seller to adjust prices up or down. There may be occasion during your sale when you glean from the traffic at your sale that your prices may be too high. Price adjustments are often made during a sale. Proper preparation can minimize this, but no one can tell you what the traffic will be like on the day and what they will or will not pay for any one item. If you have to adjust, going tag less is useful in that you won't have to run around re-tagging everything.

Finally, the idea of this strategy is to send the message to your sale-ers that everything is negotiable. Without a tag, the customer will have to ask the seller the cost and this gives the seller the opportunity to strike a bargain. If you do select this strategy, you should have a "make me an offer" mindset on all the items. Anytime you're asked about price, the response should be "make me an offer". This strategy will only be effective if you're receptive to low offers.

I can't say that I'm a fan of this strategy. I can see its advantages; however, I've been to a number of sales where there were no tags and I had to ask the seller how much an item was only to have the seller ask me to wait a moment while he/she had a mini-summit with his/her partners to discuss what price they wanted. I find this very annoying as a Sale-er and unprofessional (if you can use that term for g-sale-ing) as a Seller.

Also, you need to remember or hopefully have it written somewhere what your prices are if you do have a set price. If you don't, you run the risk of telling one Sale-er one price and another Sale-er a different price. Should the two compare notes at some stage, you may have an issue. If one paid more than another, you'll end up in an argument.

If you go with the "make me an offer" scenario, you'll have to contend with some very unappealing offers and not get upset about it. Remember you want it gone. If the offer is unacceptable, counter.

All in all. it's an interesting strategy as you can try to gauge what you might get for an item based on the customer you're engaging with. Still, it's risky and frankly, more often than not, you just appear to be unprepared and/or lazy when you don't tag your items and that's a turn-off to sale-ers.

If you are concerned about being able to adjust your prices, I have an idea that is economical, efficient and easily adjustable to your needs. Try chalkboard sandwich boards.

They are chalkboards on easels. They come in every size and shape. They are relatively cheap. You can place them on tables or wherever needed. Place them by your items and price according to what the market will bear. If you have a lot of stuff, you don't necessarily have to get 50 sandwich boards. Divide your items into sections based on price. Everything on the left is a dollar, everything on the right is five dollars, for example.

FOR A FEW DOLLARS MORE

This strategy is very popular now and involves pricing up a bit to allow room for negotiation. For example, if you want $75 for your couch, you price it at $100 hoping to get an offer for at least $75. You may even get lucky and get the full amount.

Earlier I mentioned I am selling my sectional. Well it sold. I mentioned I was hoping to get $200. I placed an ad for $250. It actually sold for full price.

You can get lucky using this method. It's rare, though. If you decide this is a good way to go for your sale, I caution you to be patient and savvy. Be careful how much you raise the price as a higher price will turn off the inexperienced Sale-er. Some people are not crazy about negotiating deals or are just naturally shy so you want to be sure you're not inadvertently turning off a potential customer.

Additionally, I want you to be aware that the experienced Sale-er knows what you're doing. Taking our $75 couch example, an experienced sale-er knows you'll take less and probably figures you'll take $75, so they offer $50. Don't get angry. They are looking for you to counter $75 and then talk you down from that price. That's just the way it's played, but in a situation like that, you can stick to your guns. If you do, you'll have to contend with the possibility that it might be the only offer you get. If you're patient and savvy, you might be able to wait for another offer. If you just want to get rid of the couch, you may want to entertain the offer, but don't be hustled into a low offer if it's not really what you want to do. I believe in rock-bottom pricing. I think we over-value our stuff. However, if you've done your homework on the real value of your stuff and you've slashed your prices to the bone, there's really no reason to take an even lower price unless you just want it out of your house.

My low baller sectional story:

I got rid of my sectional because it didn't go with anything after the kitchen remodel. The wall that separated the living room and kitchen was removed and the kitchen is just spectacular, but the living room was a disaster with its brown carpet and big brown sectional looking like a giant crap pile in the way of the view of my beautiful kitchen.

I was getting new flooring in the living room and getting rid of the ugly brown carpeting so it was the perfect time to sell the sectional. I reviewed all the ads for comparable pricing and based on just how big it is and what others were asking for smaller ones, I hit on a price of $200, I was willing to take $150 to get it out. I placed ads on OfferUp and Letgo for $250 leaving room for negotiation. I got several responses. One response came in about a day after I posted the ad and they wanted to come out right away. He was in the neighborhood and I was happy to oblige.

He came over and was rather aggressive. He liked the sectional and did the chit-chat you do when inspecting the item for sale. He asked if I could deliver it. I cannot deliver it as I have a Prius, but my neighbor, Kim has a large SUV and between the two of us, if he paid her, we could manage it.

I hesitated, at first, to reach out to Kim. I got the sense he was a time-waster. Folks, follow your gut when dealing with potential sales. If it doesn't feel right, and this goes for Sale-ers too, walk away. Your gut will tell you something is off. I'm not talking about personal safety, which of course is always a priority, I'm talking about people who just leave you with an impression that they are never going to cough up the cash.

He said he wanted it and was just concerned about the delivery, so I did reach out to Kim and she agreed if he wasn't too far. He wasn't far at all, but still I just didn't have a good feeling. Nevertheless, I relayed to him that we could deliver it. He then started negotiations on price. This is when I should have shut him down and suggested he find something else. Why? Here's the thing, if you are buying something like furniture, you should have a way to get it home. Second hand furniture isn't the same as buying from the store. Now if you need help with the delivery, and that's something the seller can offer, then you pay the full price without negotiation. I'm sorry, but you do, it's only right. In fact, you should give a bit extra for the favor. You can't expect someone to deliver furniture to you and discount it as well.

I told him that I would entertain an offer, but it would have to be reasonable. I thought perhaps he would offer me $200 and give the extra fifty to Kim for delivery. That was not what he offered. He offered $150. It's difficult not to get angry when someone is stupid and wasting your time. That's why I have every sympathy for you sellers out there when this happens to you. Nevertheless, you do need to keep your cool and focus on the goal. Remember, my goal is to get that sectional out of my house. I was considering giving it away, so any REASONABLE offer wouldn't be refused.

I was fairly annoyed with this guy to be honest. He had this gruff manner as if he was going to intimidate me. Folks I walk 4 Australian Shepherds for 3 miles every day, I'm not easily intimidated. I suggested it might be possible if he paid my neighbor $75 for the delivery. I figured if he went down on the price, I could go up for the delivery.

He said that was a good bargain and that he'd like to get it but he was checking out another sectional and he'd call me back in 20 mins. He left and I anticipated not hearing from him again. Once they're out the door, they are gone folks and so is the sale. If you've not received a deposit or some assurance that they will return, assume they will not.

Poor Kim came over to the house about ten minutes after he left. She was anticipating the move and the money. I told her he wasn't coming back. We sat and chatted a bit. I told her what he tried to pull and that he said he'd be back in twenty minutes. Twenty minutes went by and then thirty. For Kim's sake, I reached out to the guy for confirmation. He responded that he found another sectional. In fact, let me insert the actual response word for word. This is supposedly his "wife" responding to my inquiry:

He was playing me. This was his strategy and it stunk and he
stunk at it. You know, if he had been nicer and asked me for
the sectional for free, I might have given it to him. Clearly
that's what he wanted. I love to haggle and negotiate, but
there's something rather tacky about a person like this.
There's nothing wrong with trying to get the best possible
price but you don't take advantage. You stick to your word.

You do what you'll say you'll do. You treat people with respect. Sellers and Sale-ers, keep this in mind and I promise you'll do well.

After this fiasco, I'll admit to becoming a bit nervous regarding whether or not the sectional would sell. I considered lowering the price and all the things you do when you need something gone. Then one Sunday afternoon I got a response and although they were late, they did show up and the sectional is gone. For the full price, $250. Patience, courage and savvy are the key takeaways I want you to get from this story and this book. Something I still have to remind myself of on a regular basis. Oh, and I didn't have to deliver it.

As an addendum to the story, I was sans sofa, so you can imagine the hunt was on. I've been looking for some time. I needed something in gray or black. I found several things but nothing reasonable.

My floor was completed last Friday by my spectacular contractors, GTL Remodeling (If you are in the Chicagoland area, you simply have to beg them to take your job. Unless I need them, in which case don't.) My floor is so beautiful. So now my sole focus is the furniture. There was someone in my neighborhood with the exact furniture I wanted. The seller was a bit difficult to reach. I had to text several times before I got a response. Also, the price was outrageous at $600. The threshold for these types of items is about $300 on average. Still, I wanted to talk to her about it because it was the <u>exact</u> set I wanted. She said she would only be able to meet me on Sunday in the morning. I agreed, but in my head, I knew this wasn't going anywhere.

Remember I mentioned motivation? She doesn't respond to texts. She's charging $600. She can't meet me until Sunday. Does this sound like a motivated seller?

It's Saturday morning and I'm perusing the ads and what do you know, there's a nice charcoal gray sofa and loveseat set for sale for $150. It's nothing to write home about but it's just what I need. I was able to meet the seller right away and I decided to buy it. One problem, did I mention the Prius? Luckily, the seller had a truck. He was blocks away so I asked him if he wouldn't mind delivering it. He didn't mind but it would be after 5pm. Perfect!

He got to my house considerably later than 5pm but he did arrive and even helped me get it in the door. I gave him $160. Full asking and $10 additional for the trouble. I kind of thought it should be $20 additional but I didn't have the cash. And that, beloved reader, is how it's done respectfully.

Sunday morning came but I didn't reach back to the seller of the set I wanted and I didn't hear from her. Instead, I took a nap on my new/used sofa with my dogs.

FILL A BAG SALE

I once managed a resale/consignment shop in the late eighties. It was a bit upscale, but most of the stuff was just what you would find in a typical thrift store. It was part charity shop and part community consignment store. The consignment items were mainly furniture and household stuff. Typically, the consignment items came from people who were moving and didn't want to take them or sadly, they came from people who passed on and the family decided to sell the pieces.

The consignment items were given pride of place in the front of the store, the donated items took over the rest. Now, when I say took over, I mean took over. People were either incredibly generous or just needed a place to dump their crap but the crew was completely overwhelmed by the sheer amount of garbage that came in. Most of the day was spent going through all the donations. Most of it ended up as trash or donated to overseas missions. What we could sell, we did and inventory was fast becoming more than the space could bear.

We had a good amount of business but there were incredibly slow periods. Things began to come to a head as the backroom storage had boxes of merchandise that we had to stack toward the ceiling. It began to feel terribly unsafe and we already risked the wrath of the fire marshal. Drastic action was needed. The team brainstormed and we came up with a marketing stunt, $5 bag sale day. We had the customer bring in their own bag or we would provide them with one and they could stuff the bag with all they wanted for $5. It was, of course, confined to the donated items and not the consignment.

We planned ahead and had a countdown clock marking the days, as you would do with Christmas, to build excitement. We placed ads in the free recycler paper. We posted signs near the road for the passing traffic to see. It was a lot of work and a lot of fun.

It was extremely successful. As you can imagine the baby and kid clothes were the first to go. But all the little knick-knacks, costume jewelry, toys, games, dishes, even the pictures on the walls were flying out the door. We still had plenty of inventory, but it went a long way toward clearing it out.

After the big sale the staff, me included, considered doing it on a weekly or monthly basis. But clearly that wasn't sustainable and the reason we got the business we did was because it was something special.

Did we lose money on the bag sale? We didn't get as much as we could have selling the individual pieces. We sold onesies, for example, at $.25 each. Twenty onesies would be $5 and perhaps you could get twenty-five onesies in a bag. But when inventory gets as large as it did, it begins to cost you money rather than making you money. So, thinking big picture, it was the smart move.

The 'bag sale' could be a successful strategy for your sale if:

- You have a ton of small stuff
- You want to get rid of everything fast
- You don't mind things selling for less

This strategy is particularly successful for those multi-family sales. There's always a ton of little items from shower curtain rings to a bag of nails. Tons of toys and of course, clothes. I want to talk about clothes at sales in depth, but in this case, I'm talking about baby and kid clothes. The bag sale strategy is going to save you time and energy and most importantly, save you from tagging everything. The downside is that you will not make as much as if you sold everything individually. As with any strategy, you'll weigh the risks versus the rewards and decide what works best for you.

If you do decide to do a bag sale, be sure to advertise well. We'll get in-depth with advertising shortly, but try to build excitement around the idea. You want your sale-er to think: "Wow look at all the stuff I can get for just $5!"

App Selling Strategy – "Ooops Wrong Number"

This is a bonus strategy I use when selling on the various online apps. I'm including it because it's very effective and gets items sold fast.

I came up with this idea when I was selling an old iPhone on OfferUp. I was getting slammed with responses and my phone would not stop pinging. Most of the offers were low ball nonsense. Some were genuinely interested. Some others still were genuinely interested but slow to react. These were people who wanted to pay full asking, but couldn't commit to a meeting time/place. I decided to "confuse" my text responses. I did this by "accidently" sending messages to the wrong person. For example; if I got an offer for full price but the person couldn't make it until the weekend, I would "accidentally" send a message like:

> "Sure, I could meet you in an hour."

The response would come back:

> "No, no, I can't meet in an hour, I said on Saturday."

My response would be:

> "OMG, I'm so sorry, that was supposed to be for someone else. UGH! I've got too many responses. Sure, if I still have it, I can meet you on Saturday. SORRY ☹."

Or if I got a low-ball offer:

"Sorry, I can't hold it, I've gotten a huge response. It has to be first come first serve. "

Low ball Response:

My response:

Huh?

"Oh geez! SORRY, wrong person."

The iPhone sold for the asking price about two hours after it was posted.

This strategy is workable whether you have a big response or not. It's also workable the from the buyer's point of view:

Yes, $200 is great! There's someone closer that I've been chatting with but her price is higher. I think I can make it in an hour if that works for you?

I didn't agree to $200.

What?

Oh crap, I'm sorry that text was for someone else.

How embarrassing! (wink)

As with every strategy, there's a risk it won't work, but strangely I've never found any strategy more effective than competition. When I was selling the iPhone, I met the buyer

at my local 7-11. They were practically speeding to meet me.
I was surprised at how effective this strategy was and I've
used it on several occasions. I used this strategy on the
sectional. Advising any inquiries that I had several
interested parties. This doesn't always work. It didn't work
on several people who inquired. But then it did.

You don't have to have a lot of inquiries to tell people that
you do. Make up a text that makes little sense to the
recipient and when you get a response for clarification,
simply advise them that the text was meant for someone else.

The reason this strategy is in my arsenal is that when it
comes to the apps, you get an extraordinary number of time-
wasters. People who think they want what you have but just
aren't ready to pull the trigger. Part of the reason is because
the object is just a picture on a screen. There's a lot to be
said for being able to hold something in your hand. I think
Amazon may have a lot of this as well, People who look at
something and think they want it, but they just can't press
the "Checkout" button. How many times have you added
something to your cart and then just left it?

I consider this strategy similar to the "Last One" tags on
Amazon or eBay. Something to motive the Seller or Sale-er
on the other end to pull the trigger.

I have a couple of metal detectors. The kind you use on the
beach trying to find coins and rings. I don't use them. It was
a dumb idea. I used one once and found about a dollar in
change and then I had to have it. I had a real bug up my butt
about metal detectors for a long time.

I finally decided to post one of them. It's the lower end one. I
posted it for $35 expecting to get $25-30. It's been up on the

sites for months. I get responses on a fairly regular basis. All of whom want it for less than I will accept. Offers of $10 or $20. It sells for about $100 and frankly, it's not taking up any space so I can wait for the right offer. Occasionally, I get an offer for the full price. I say great, when can you meet? "Well, maybe tomorrow or how about the weekend?" This is a time-waster. Sending me the offer was the equivalent of adding the metal detector to his shopping cart but never intending to buy. The "Ooops" strategy was born out of this experience. If the person thinks there's a rush on your item, they tend to either commit or go away. Both results work in your favor.

CHAPTER 5. ADVERTISING

Getting the word out about your sale isn't limited to a sign on the corner these days. The street I live on is on a T-junction so putting a sign on the corner would only get me the audience that lives on that street. When it's time for your sale, make sure to plan out your advertising as carefully as you plan the sale itself.

Advertising is probably the costliest part of holding a sale. You can buy signs at a dollar store or Walmart, but they don't catch the eye and we do want to keep the overhead costs for this sale to a minimum. Here are some ideas with regards to signage:

1) Recycle!! Ask your neighbors for their signs. They may want to keep them but if they don't mind you can reuse the signs even if they've written their address on them. Get a bottle of lighter fluid or goof off. Spray a bit on a cloth and wipe off the address.

Be careful as this will take off everything including Garage Sale.

2) Reuse campaign signs! I like campaign signs much better than garage sale signs. They're bigger, their everywhere come election time and they can be spray painted. Same technique to remove the text from the sign. If you don't want to bother, just get some spray paint to cover the original and a contrasting color to let the world know.

3) If you get a large number of signs, try...painting....one...word...on.....each.....sign. Then, when placing the signs, place them in the order of the sentence. Ex: You....are.....a block.....away....from the....Garage Sale.....of the....Year....Turn Now!

4) Ask local shop owners if you can place a sign in their window. This is old school but still effective.

5) Grocery store notice boards are great places to place a flyer. Many stores have stopped having boards, sadly, but if yours does it will typically be on a wall near the door.

6) Don't wash the car! Write on your car with a bingo dauber or car marker. You've seen this at weddings or sporting events. People write on their car: "Congrats Jack & Jill" or "My sport team is better than yours" You get the point. Why not treat your sale like it's a sporting event? "Follow me to the Garage Sale of the Year" or "Garage Sale Bliss can be found at (address)" Bingo daubers wash off if you cannot find the car markers.

7) Anything can be a sign. You can build your own sign out of just about anything. Take a look in your garage for an old piece of wood. Maybe an old shelf, a drawer or piece of paneling. If you don't have anything, check a neighbor. Spray paint it with your

details. I will tell you, neatness counts on these art projects. If it looks sloppy or they can't tell what your sign says, you're better off buying something.

ONLINE/DIGITAL ADVERTISING

As I mentioned, I live on a street with a T-junction at the end which prevents access from the main road. It can be quite nice really. It's mostly quiet. I have a few nut case neighbors but for the most part it's idyllic. Except when it comes to garage sales. It's very difficult to get all but the most serious Sale-ers to venture from the main road to our little enclave. This means that we get just the neighbors walking past. It limits the audience considerably.

Every year our township attempts a town garage sale weekend, typically around Memorial Day weekend, which is nice because it also happens to be my birthday. I enjoy walking the dogs and seeing what's for sale, but the numbers of families participating seems to be dwindling every year. I think this is because of our lack of traffic. There are several other factors which I will get into in another chapter, but one of the biggest reasons is the lack of traffic. There's only one way to combat the traffic issue and that's to advertise. For our township, the advertising extends to a message on the community sign in front of their office. There's nothing wrong with this advertising. Many of the community residents wouldn't know it was going on if they didn't put it on the sign. Still, I think they could do better. I would have them ask residents who will be participating and putting together a map. Then add to the sign that maps are available in the office. This would go a long way toward driving traffic. They also have access to the town website, which would be a great way to pull everyone in and really do the event properly. But besides an ad on the board, there's not much more attention given to it. When it comes to advertising our town garage sale, it's really up to us as individual sellers to get the word out.

So, what do you do? If you're lucky/unlucky enough to live somewhere with a lot of traffic, perhaps you don't really need to advertise much. Wrong. The key isn't so much about the traffic as it is the right traffic. If you're in a spot without a huge amount of traffic, maybe you should take out an ad in the paper. Wrong. Bless the poor newspaper people but those days are over and we want to keep our costs low. Preferably, net zero overhead is our target. We need to get the word out. Our goal is: 1) the right audience, 2) the most traffic, 3) for little or no out of pocket cost.

We need to place ads on the internet, but in strategic places. Advertise to an audience within a 20-mile radius. No one is going to drive more than twenty miles to get to your garage sale. They probably won't drive 10 miles, however, if they are in the neighborhood or if they have errands, family or friends in the neighborhood, you may have a potential Sale-er so we want to be sure to get the word out. But the question is where?

1. Craigslist – That's kind of a no-brainer isn't it? But the CL isn't what it once was. People access the internet mainly on their phone and the CL isn't really mobile friendly. Classifieds 2.0 has optimized it for your phone, which is really what keeps the CL relevant. Also, CL is trying to monetize itself now, so you can't just post anything for free. As of my writing this, you can still post a Garage Sale ad for free. For the serious Sale-er looking for a good sale, CL is still the first place to check. Tip: If your house is a bit

difficult to find, add a little Google map of your location or picture of your house. Don't assume everyone has GPS or that it works getting to your house. For years my GPS said I lived at a flooring store. I'm not sure where the flooring store was as there isn't a flooring store in my neighborhood. But according to the map, that's where I lived. It only corrected itself this year. Good thing I know my way home.

2. Apps – OfferUp and Letgo are your second stop for free advertising. This is a last-minute advertising task for you. The reason is, you want your ad to be at the top of the page and it won't be for long. If you place an ad a week before, no one will see it on the day of unless they looked for garage sales, which isn't likely. On the day of your sale, once the tables are all set up, take a picture of your set-up and use it when posting your ad. It also helps to have a nice Garage Sale sign in the picture itself so people can see at a glance what your ad is all about. These apps are driven by pictures, so you'll want to make it very clear. Perhaps take a picture of the garage sale sign and post that as the first image. Next tip, when posting your ad, put some keywords in. These are words that will respond to search. For example, if you have a stereo for sale at your garage sale, at the bottom of your ad write stereo. You could conceivably put your whole inventory in the ad but keep it to the eye catcher items at your sale. You'll have to use your phone to post the ad so you don't want to write everything you have for sale. If someone is looking for a stereo, your garage sale ad will pop up. Ta Da! Another shiny new Sale-er

3. Ugh, Facebook. Ok full disclosure, I'm not a Facebook user anymore. I had an ugly incident when my beloved Lucy had puppies and I was trying to find homes for them. So why am I recommending Facebook to you? Well, I do so reluctantly. I'm suggesting it because there are sale pages on FB just for your neighborhood. This is a great way to get the word out and drive the traffic your way. I do need to say, however, please be careful especially sharing your address. I never had a moments trouble with Facebook until I did.

Please be careful with any online app or service. When you post, you'll naturally post your address, it is a garage sale, but if you're uncomfortable for any reason, get a bit creative. Consider having people reach out to you for the address.

"Want to know where the best garage sale of the year is going to be?" PM me!

This way you have some contact with the people who are coming to your home. In the end, just trust your gut and you won't go wrong.

New Apps

I've recently found some new apps for finding sales. They don't have a huge audience yet, but don't discount them. For Sale-ers and sellers alike, the app world is the future of garage sale-ing. Increasingly, people want to be able to just pull out their phone and find what they want with a couple of swipes. You shouldn't rely solely on these apps but for now, add them to your phone and check them regularly. If you find they are not helpful, you can always take them off. Here's the lowdown on the best of them:

Yard Sale Treasure Map

This app is actually pretty cool, although at first you're going to be less than impressed. This App draws ads from Craigslist so you may think, "Well, I've already got Classifieds 2.0 so why do I need Yard Sale Treasure Map?" The difference is that the app pulls just from the garage sales on CL and plots them on the map. If you "star" the places you'd like to visit, it will plan out your route as well. Note that this only works if the CL ad has an address. You may not get all the garage sales in the area if the post doesn't contain an address. Also, you cannot post from the app. You must go on CL to post your ad.

I really like this app. It's limited in some ways, but I like the idea of plotting the sales on a map. I find it incredibly helpful to have a map of all the sales you want to visit in the palm of your hand. For Sellers, this can be very helpful to you in getting traffic to your location. Note that this app is still in its early days, so you may not have the world beating a path to your door right away. The real advantage to this app is having all the sales in an area on a map; or at least the ones that have posted on Craigslist. Sellers, make sure you post on Craigslist and include your address so that you'll be featured on the app as well.

Gsalr.com

If you're a Sale-er, you probably know about Gsalr.com. It's been around a while. The name is terrible so it doesn't really get the attention it should. What's worse is they make you sign up before you can post your ad. This would be fairly innocuous as you have to sign up for most anything nowadays, but Gsalr makes it near impossible. There's always some issue with your sign up. Typically, it's the password. You do what it tells you and still there's some kind of problem.

Well now they have an app. Same problems, different format. I tried to sign up and it still doesn't like any one of the 50 passwords I tried. I cannot recommend this app. I had high hopes for it. The app, like the Yard Sale app, shows sales on a map format. The issue is, you cannot really be sure where they get their information. I assume that the ads are posted by users, but since everyone seems to have so much trouble signing up, I wonder.

Bottom-line: Sale-ers, it might be worth it to see what's happening in your neighborhood. Sellers, just take a pass on this app.

5 miles (looks like Smiles)

This is a new app that seems to want to be everything to everyone. It has auctions like Deal Dash, For Sale items like OfferUp & Letgo, and community, services, housing, etc. listings like CL. It might be a bit too much, but I do like the app a lot. It's got listing categories that other sites do not have. You CAN post from the app, which is fantastic. They do not appear to pull from other sites so you will need to post directly.

The drawbacks are two in particular; I think the app needs to focus a bit and not try to meet every need. It needs streamlining. I think they are trying to be like Amazon for the secondary market, but the "bid ads" and then the "for sale" ads make it rather distracting. The app is designed well once you get used to it. There are links at the top and bottom of the screen to get you to where you want to be.

They have a page devoted to "Yard Sales" which is their category for everything g-sale related. There are ads for Moving Sales, Garage Sales and some just posting objects for sale. The good news is that the ads don't seem to expire. This is also the bad news. I saw one sale that looked pretty interesting but it was in June and its now November.

Bottom-line: I like this app. It could prove very useful for both Sellers and Sale-ers. There's no map per se, but the ads do show a map of where the sale is located. It's worth a try. It's not extremely popular yet, so don't rely on it solely, but every ad potentially drives traffic. Sale-ers, there's a lot to look at on this app but probably worth the time.

NextDoor

Of all the apps out there, I find myself on this app most. NextDoor is a neighborhood app. It's all the news and nonsense going on in YOUR neighborhood. It also has some great ads, the usual "for sale" ads but they have a category for Garage Sales. It takes a minor bit of digging to find but the sales are strictly in your neighborhood. The ads don't have an expiry date and there are ads in the wrong category. You can post directly in the app. They do not draw from other sites so you would have to post there.

The drawbacks are few; the digging to find the garage sale category and the number of users on the app. I have to say, I kind of love this app. I love the idea of chatting and getting to know the neighbors. Neighbors looking out for neighbors and, most importantly, keeping our dollars in the neighborhood. Bottom-line: Good app for sales and great app for neighborhood insights.

I've recently found some interesting websites specifically designed to help you find the G-Sales in your neighborhood. The popularity of these sites can't really be measured, unlike the apps where you can see how many people have downloaded and/or rated it. However, if we're attempting to get the word out about our sale, or indeed trying to find the sale of the century, no stone should be left unturned. Here are some promising options:

Garage Sale Finder.com

It's not very mobile friendly, it is similar to Gsalr and Yard Sale treasure map, just for browsers. It offers an option to sign up and get notifications sent to you about new sales, which I find very enticing. Advertising is free but you will have to provide your information. The site gets its revenue from paid advertisers.

You'll enter your zip code or the zip code where you want to find sales and the sales will appear on the map. It's not clear whether or not they pull ads from other sites, but I think they must. The map idea is a fantastic way to display ads, especially for Sale-ers. I suspect that since the model is the same or similar to the other apps mentioned, the sites and apps may be owned by the same entity. I say this because I found the same ads on all the different platforms. But that doesn't necessarily mean I'm right or that it's a problem. I mention this only so you don't think you must subscribe to everything in order to find sales. Now if you're a Seller, you'll probably want to post everywhere they will allow you to do so. It just makes sense. But I have a sneaking suspicion that if you post on one of these sites, they will appear magically on another similar site. Check before you post and save a few keystrokes.

Gsalr.com

I won't go over again the issues with this site. If you can post on it, by all means do so. I don't think this site gets a ton of traffic and it is terribly difficult to use, but try it and maybe your luck will be better than most.

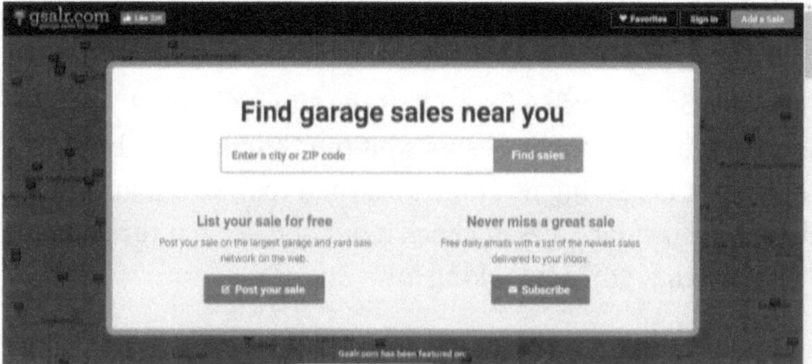

Yard Sale Search.com

Here again is another map-based search. I think when you visit these sites you'll find they are the browser-based versions of the apps I've outlined previously. For those who find it easier to post online versus the app, this might be the better option. When you post your ad, choose one of the options and then check the other sites listed to see if the ad is picked up by the other sites. I've found that the same ads seem to be posted in all the sites and I think they feed off each other. If so, you'll save yourself some time and effort.

With Yard Sale Search, I found that the site looks very "homemade". It actually seems a bit too "homemade" but in the interest of leaving no stone unturned to find that amazing sale or spectacular Sale-er, check it out and see if it turns out to be just what you are looking for.

Facebook Garage Sale Finder

Oh joy, FB has a garage sale finder. Well actually, Garage Sale Finder.com has a Facebook page. It's just another way to review the site. If you're a Facebook fan, this is a terrific option.

As mentioned previously, Facebook has pages devoted to local sales, so you should definitely check out those pages if you are a FB user. I would be remiss if I didn't say again, please be careful. I found these pages fantastic, until the ugliness showed up. There are trolls on these pages. They are not just your neighbors. Be very careful about what you put online. Okay, my mom hat is now off.

OTHER ADVERTISING OPTIONS

I've shared with you the most common places to advertise your sale or find a great sale. But there are other, less common ways of getting the word out that might make all the difference in turnout for your sale.

Community Websites:

Humans are tribal and we tend to organize and create community where there was none. Think carefully about the organizations or communities you belong to, even if the connection is rather loose:

- Township
- School District
- Synagogue, Church or Parish
- Block Club
- Park District
- Precinct

We have 4 different townships in my neighborhood and apparently, I belong to all of them. I once called for a particular issue and was referred to another local township. Apparently, they all overlap each other and services are shared amongst them. My point is, there are organizations in your world that you may belong to just because of where you live. These organizations, whatever they are, have websites and offices that could help you get the word out. Ask them to post an announcement on their website. Don't get upset if you receive push back. This won't be your main source of advertising. But also, don't take no for an answer. If you're persistent and persistently nice, you'll tend to get the result you want. They may want you to pay a fee. If it's not too much and you can manage it within your budget, by all means. Obviously, we hope for a zero-overhead sale, but you also need to weigh the cost vs. rewards. If your township is waiving sale permit fees but needs to charge you $20 for an ad, well that doesn't seem outrageous to me. Now if that same township gets no traffic to their website, then $20 is not going to get you much. My township HQ is run very well but their website leaves a lot to be desired. I would not consider paying for an ad on their website. These are the factors you should consider if you decide to pay for advertising.

If your organization is insistent upon compensation and you don't think it worth the money, ask them if they would consider allowing you to post a flyer. This isn't a request that is normally turned down, but if they do turn it down, don't despair. More than likely, they aren't a very nice group of folks and thereby won't have a lot of traffic anyway.

In this chapter, I've shared with you the ways and methods of advertising your sale. But these are just some of the options available to you. Try to come up with creative solutions to get the word out there. Whether you are on a busy thoroughfare or a tiny cul de sac, getting the word out is key to the success of any sale.

Chapter 6. What NOT to Sell at your Sale

Gentle reader, welcome to the chapter that started it all. This is the chapter which motivated me to write this book. I've been Sale-ing for decades but the last few years, with the few exceptions I've already mentioned, have just been a disaster. I'm just stunned at what people will put out at a sale. There were times when I wondered if they just opened the garbage bin and dumped the contents on a table.

I do believe that there is usually a buyer for pretty much anything. The only real difficulty is finding that buyer. Even at the sales where I just wanted to scream. The sellers just didn't reach their target audience. What they were selling wasn't garage sale stuff, but they promoted themselves as having a Garage Sale.

I mentioned previously that there is nothing more annoying for a Sale-er than going to a sale that is a complete waste of time. In this chapter I'm going to address some key mistakes that sellers make in the actual merchandise they have to sell. Most of these mistakes are just about not knowing the audience. When you're determining what you have for sale, ask yourself, "who is going to buy this?" "Who is looking for this item?" Knowing this and then marketing to that particular audience is key. That is why this book addresses creating an inventory and knowing your buyer first. But now that we've learned a bit and we've got our inventory, let's take a look at that inventory in depth and with a critical eye.

DONATE YOUR CLOTHES AND SELL YOUR STUFF

Oh, here comes the rant: In my neighborhood, the word garage sale can mean just about anything, but in particular, annoyingly, it means clothes. I've said before that the name your sale has sets an expectation of what will be at the sale. Garage sale denotes things that might be stored in a garage. It's entirely possible that you would store old clothes in your garage, but it's not advisable as they would be pretty icky after a couple of weeks.

Honestly the clothes issue is the most frustrating, exasperating and annoying issue with the sales in my neighborhood. It's every sale in the neighborhood as well. When it comes to baby and kid clothes, honestly, that's not an issue. If you've got kids growing out of things faster than you can buy them, it only makes sense. What I'm talking about are the adult clothes. Who is wearing other people's clothes? Besides the gross factor, the general rule of thumb is, donate your clothes and sell your stuff. It's so aggravating to anticipate a good sale and get nothing but other people's DNA laden clothes. Stop it.

When you go to a garage sale, you expect to find tools, small appliances, knick-knacks, toys, etc. You do not expect to find racks and racks of clothing. (Oh yeah, just down the street from my house.) If there is clothing, you expect it to be kids clothing, baby onesies and the like and even for these sales, you should be really clear on what you have to offer. I don't want your baby clothes and if that's all you have, it would be nice to have your advertising reflect that. What you don't expect is adult wear. I wish I had taken a picture of the one this summer. There was nothing but racks chock-full of clothes on hangers. The sign said garage sale and since the location was accurate, I guess you had to say they didn't exactly lie, but UGH, I was annoyed.

First off, used clothing is gross. It's gross when you buy it at Goodwill and it's gross when you buy it for your kids. People do buy it. When I was a teen, I shopped exclusively at the thrift stores. Growing up all my Marcia Brady dresses came from the church rummage sale. It's what you do when you're young and broke or a single mom on a budget. That's the way things work. Just not at a garage sale.

Please donate your clothes. The charities that accept clothing donations, really need those clothes. Most of those clothes never make it to the shop floor, by the way. Much of the clothing you donate gets shipped to impoverished nations. Ever wonder how a poor young Kenyan child got a t-shirt from Disney World? Now there's a lot of debate about whether this is a good thing or not. Our used clothing does depress Kenya's own textile industry. By the same token, a person in Nairobi selling our donated clothes can make about $10 a day which is actually a living wage in that part of the world so it's difficult to make a judgement on the practice. I know that if my old clothes can make a difference in someone's life on the other side of the globe, sorry no-brainer.

All that aside, when you go garage sale-ing, you are not shopping for clothes. While you may entertain the notion of getting something for your two-year-old, buying someone's negligée (oh yeah at a sale last summer) for yourself is just not going to happen. I'm sure it's very clean, but you know, gross.

Now, if you advertise a clothing sale; I mean you put on the sign, SECOND-HAND CLOTHING SALE, I have no complaints.

But if you advertise it as a garage sale and it turns out to be just all your fat clothes, I'm not going to love ya. Now the problem with that is that I tell two friends and they tell two friends and so on and so on and so on. It's not cool to tick off your Sale-ers. You don't want to waste your time or that of your sale-er. If you simply must sell your old clothes, be clear about what you have. I realize there is a market for these items. People in my neighborhood wouldn't do it, if there wasn't a buyer. But more often than not, the sellers are sitting there without anything being sold. Think about it, would you go to a garage sale looking for clothes?

FLEA MARKETS

A real option for the clothing inspired among you is the flea market. You can devote an entire booth to your clothes if you like, but I would suggest you have something else because again people aren't coming to the flea market for clothes. But at the flea market people expect to see all kinds of stuff, so you might do very well. It will cost you something up front, but it's not a bad way to make a little extra change. If you don't have a lot of items or the up-front money makes you nervous, consider going in with a friend or neighbor and splitting the cost of the booth.

BITS AND BOBS

I'm calling this section bits and bobs because there's really no other name for it. This is the 12 pack of curtain rings, the broken bits of jewelry, the old "People" magazines and the things people have to ask you to find out what it is.

Let me be clear, if these things are in your sale, throw them out. If they can't be thrown out, put them in a free box. If you really think it's saleable, I mean YOU would definitely buy it at a garage sale, Ok, but please make sure these kinds of things are a small part of the sale and not the main event. You Sale-ers out there know exactly what I'm talking about. A whole table full of ceramic Santas and pencil holders and adjustable size rings. Maybe there's a collector out there but then those are best posted online.

Again, there is a buyer for pretty much anything you want to sell, but finding that buyer is key. It's no good hoping the buyer for your troll doll collection will just happen by your yard sale. These items are best put sold digitally. Remember what I said about doing your research. If these small items are really worth something, chances are they'll be online. Do the searches, Google, Letgo, CL, eBay. What are they worth? Is it worth the eBay fee?

Where I'm going with this is simple, I want you to have the sale of the century. These little bits of clutter can really throw you off the path to profitability. Your sale-ers come and see what you have and it leaves them with an impression. If you've got a table of non-functional junk, it says something you probably don't want it to say. It says waste of time, waste of money, nothing but junk. That's really what we want to avoid. So bottom-line, toss this kind of stuff, if you really don't want it. Now, I'm all about the recycle, so if you don't want it in a landfill, I completely concur. There are lots of possibilities for the small items that fill our lives that don't involve trashing them. Do you have a creative mind? Can you make something new out of them? What about a troll wreath for your front door? Anything can be made into something new with a glue gun and a bit of inspiration.

If you're not creative or just don't have that ambition, consider options like Freecycle. Freecycle is a group on

Yahoo where people give away items that still have some use. Some items have no use, but it doesn't end up in a landfill and that's the point. Freecycle can be a bit ugly. People put up wanted ads, which I find unacceptable really. Example, a person put up a wanted ad for something I just happened to have. It wasn't cheap, but I wasn't using it and if they really needed it, I didn't have a problem letting it go. I responded letting them know I had it but I would need some compensation for it if they indeed wanted it. I didn't demand a price, whatever they would have offered, I would have accepted. They responded with a diatribe I would not repeat in this space. They even reported me to the moderator. The moderator gave me a "warning". Honestly, I don't know what world some people live in. My point is, as with all the digital space, be very careful.

I brought up the "free box" earlier, this is a box you have at your sale with just items you want gone. It's a very popular idea lately. I've seen these at most of the sales over the last few years. I don't think this drives traffic of any kind, but it's a very good way to get rid of the fluff stuff in your sale that will have a tough time finding a buyer.

Donation options are abundant in most places. I hesitate with offering this as a first option. Why? Having worked at thrift store, I know a bit about the donation cycle. If your items are just fluff. I mean they really don't serve a purpose and there's little to no value, they may end up in a landfill anyway. The reason is simple, retail space has a value. You might think your Santa statue is adorable, but if it's not Christmas, the store really can't store it until it is. Your curtain rings are indeed useful, but is anyone coming to Goodwill for curtain rings? The store considers these things when they're placing items on the floor for sale. They need things that will move. Certain things move but others don't and all things take up space so chances are if you can't sell it at your sale, neither can they. Still there's an off-chance that they can ship it to another location or an outlet store. Somethings will end up in other countries. It's possible, but be aware if you're trying to avoid these objects ending up in a landfill, donating them won't necessarily spare them that fate.

OTHER "NOTS"

Did you know that it could be against the law in your state to sell a second-hand mattress? There are restrictions on selling of second-hand bedding. Most of the laws are written for the retailer and not the private re-seller, so you don't actually know for sure what the rules are for you.

To be sure, there aren't any mattress police running around looking for people that are selling their mattresses. But there are solid health concerns with used bedding. I even question buying a comforter or bedspread, but those you can wash. The mattress, not so much, but if you Sale-ers are shopping for a used mattress, you can steam them before using. That might be more work than it's worth. I think the concerns are mostly around bedbugs, which are very hard to get rid of apparently.

When I think about it, a used mattress does sound pretty gross. We sleep in hotels and B&Bs and I think that normalizes it, but I doubt the hotels are steam cleaning the mattresses after the last guest leaves. Considering all that happens on a mattress, and no I'm not going blue here, pets, babies, people's coats, food, accidents and yes, all the other things that happen. It's probably about as sanitary as your toilet. So maybe you skip the used buy/sell.

Another big NOT is weapons. This should be fairly obvious, but then again, some people voted for Trump, so let's not rely on the obvious and spell it out. No guns, knives (weapon knives), throwing stars, nun chucks etc. Defensive weaponry, like pepper spray and stun guns can't be sold without a license and you really don't want to sell this kind of stuff at a garage sale. The hunting knives tend to be okay, but honestly, I wouldn't. If there's a question about its legality, just take it out of the sale. It's not worth it. Let's say you have some nun chucks you want to sell. Your sale is going along just fine and a little kid who just discovered Bruce Lee is there and sees the nun chucks. He starts picking them up and playing with them. His mother sees this and freaks. Rightfully so since it is decidedly not a toy. She may complain to you or worse she doesn't complain to you. She goes to the police and tells them you have weapons at your garage sale. That's going to get them to your house. Now if you're lucky the officer just tells you to put them away. If you're not lucky, the officer might ask what other weapons you have. Really unlucky, you might have a fine. Still, it's a lot better than that kid hitting himself in the head with those things. Try to think about any possible repercussions and err toward caution.

Our next NOT is SHOES! I'm sorry, I am completely stunned at the number of shoes I have seen at these sales. Come on, SHOES? Maybe you don't agree with me that the used clothes thing is pretty gross, but surely, we can all agree on the shoes, right? I have best friends that I've known for centuries and would give my life for and I'm not putting on their shoes. And I just want to say, these are not the most attractive shoes. I've seen people trying to sell trainers after clearly a lot of wear, they throw them in the washer and then the dryer so when you see them they resemble more closely a ball of wadded plastic more than a shoe. It's stunningly gross, Throw the shoes out. It's not hygienic to wear other people's shoes. Okay rant over, besides I'm starting to itch thinking about this.

Okay, my final NOT is periodicals and books. I'm kind of on the fence about this. I like cookbooks and I tend to pick up a lot of these at garage sales. The periodicals, I can kind of understand. It's dumb and you have to be the kind of person that really likes that stuff. I do, when I was a kid I used to collect all old Beatle magazines and comic books and newspapers. I've always been an antique fan, it's just that my taste in antiques is toward the worthless. These things don't make any money. I saved the newspaper from Nelson Mandela being freed and when Fred Astaire died. No one wants that stuff but me.

Here's a funny story. As you know, after a long drought, the Chicago Cubs won the world series. For years I said that if they won it would mark the beginning of the apocalypse and then Trump won, so you tell me. But everyone in my beloved Chicago was over the moon about the Cubs. I personally was pleased but to be honest, I don't care. There was a run on the newspapers in our city, the Chicago Sun-Times and the Tribune. They wanted that headline, "World Series Champs." I really feel bad for the newspaper business. People who wouldn't buy the paper to line their bird cage were buying this issue and the newspapers just couldn't keep up. Well bless the secondary market because all you needed to do was open your favorite app and there were fifty opportunities to buy the papers and the price just went through the roof. I saw an ad $400 for one paper. Yeah, it got that insane.

I knew the price spike would fall dramatically. People don't want to pay $.50 for a paper, they're aren't going to pay $50 no matter what's going on. Sure enough, the price dropped like a brick. Now this is what the price is like for both papers and it's not selling.

It's kind of sad, really. If you're a history geek, like I am, you might think it sad as well. But the truth is most people see newspaper collecting as just a fire hazard.

If you've decided to try and sell your periodicals, okay but put them on a digital platform not your garage sale. If you can. take the best offer you get. If they don't sell, recycle them and try not to tear up. It's a strange world trying to figure out the things we value.

These are my key "WHAT NOT TO SELL" items, but there are a lot more. Candles, stuffed animals, old TVs or Monitors (CRTs), VHS and DVDs (folks you might get something on the DVDs but no one has a VHS anymore we stream everything now). You'll know the real turn-offs at a garage sale right away just based on traffic. If you find during your sale that some items just really aren't getting any attention, have a free box nearby and slide the items into them.

WHEN NOT TO SELL

We talked about the items that are better left out of your sale, the WHAT not to sell. Now let's talk about WHEN. There is a trend now that sales open on Fridays in the summer and don't open on Sundays. I think there must be a rumor going around that everyone has Fridays off in the summer. If that's true, I didn't get the memo. I'm not sure where that idea came from, but I would very much like it to STOP. I can't tell you how many times I've gone to sales looking for something in particular only to be told, "oh, we had it on Friday," As much as sale-ers love sale-ing, very few of us can afford to lose a day's pay to do it.   The truth is, the first day of a sale is critical. All the good stuff anyone wants is gone on the first day. It really burns me when I find out Saturday Morning that the sale was open Friday. I used to stop going to sales if I discovered they were open on Friday. It's just a waste of time. I'm just looking for a fair shot at everything. If you value our friendship, please don't open on Fridays. Set up on Friday. Do your dress rehearsal on Friday, just don't open.

Sunday is a spectacular day to hold a sale and yet, very few sellers actually do. I don't know if they're opening on Friday or what, but the sale-ers are looking for you, open up!

Chapter 7. Let's Talk about the Weather

As I've mentioned, my home is in the suburbs of my beloved Chicago. One of the many things Chicago is known for is its weather. It's hardly as dramatic as people make it out to be. Honestly, we kvetch about it more than anyone and still we'd live nowhere else. I think you have to be born here to love it as we do. But that doesn't mean the weather can't ruin our plans now and again. What happens when you go through all

the trouble of planning your sale and the weather turns
against you? Well I have some ideas for you, Chicago-style!

A Sale for all Seasons

Garage sales happen to be a kind of seasonal event where I
live. Obviously, with our weather, you want to plan for a day
that is going to be sunny and lovely. Typically, the sales start
around Memorial Day for the bravest amongst us, because
Memorial Day can be a bit tricky. I mentioned my birthday
falls during this time. It once snowed on my birthday. It's
usually ok, a bit rainy, maybe a bit chilly. Rain or shine
though, people put out their wares. The season ends
typically by early November. Yes, even in November you can
find a sale. We really don't let the weather stop us. So how
do we do it? Well, it's mostly our culture. But there are
things you can do if the weather turns fickle. Clearly you
want to have a good idea of the forecast, but that won't
always save you. The importance of having a plan B can't be
understated. Typically, sales in our neck of the woods keep
tarps nearby each table. When the rain starts, the tarps come
out. Everyone helps including the customers. This exact
scenario happened this summer at a very nice sale.

It was the middle of summer and they just got hit with a
crappy day. Sometimes this just can't be avoided. What do
you do? You've planned this for a month, you've set the date.
This particular sale was a multi-family and the proceeds
went to a charity so they really were up a creek without a
paddle.

When I arrived, the weather was still okay. I was coming
back from walking the dogs and spotted the sale. All of a
sudden, the weather turned dreadful. The winds started first

and then the rain. Characteristically, the tarps came out and almost took off like a parachute, once the wind took hold of them. It was all hands-on deck as the rain followed and four of us grabbed the edges of the tarps and started covering everything. The textiles, arts, and electronics went back in the garage. The garden items, like a leaf blower and a smoker grill stayed out but the boxes they were in were covered by the tarp. The organizers of this sale were especially smart and had a mini party tent that they remained under. I was a bit worried that the wind might take it away, but it was well secured. Once everything was covered and secured, I carried on shopping.

You can't control the weather but you can plan for it. The key items they had were clear tarps or drop cloths, bungees to secure them, the canopy to protect everyone and the ability to move the items that couldn't get wet fairly quickly. Where they could have done better was the layout itself. Really anything that can't get wet should stay in the garage. Electronics, textiles, art, books, anything that would be damaged by being wet, should remain in your garage if at all possible. Or at the very least these items should be easily moveable back into the garage.

PLAN FOR EVERYTHING

The impossible is not impossible when planning an event. You will have to learn to go with the flow. Don't fight it. Don't get crazy. Just embrace the chaos. There are going to be things that you just don't think of, don't panic; just adjust. Weather may be the least of the things that don't go according to plan. Just try to plan as much as you can and as much as your budget will allow.

A canopy is a really good idea if you can manage it. Even if you're in a heatwave, both you and your sale-ers will welcome the relief of a good-sized canopy. Clearly, you'll want to minimize your costs, but I suggest looking on one of the sites or apps mentioned earlier for a used one. I found several on OfferUp. One in

particular was a nice party one with walls. It's a bit of an investment to be sure but I think you'll find another use for it at some point, barbeques, picnics or a smoker's tent during a holiday party.

Another great option, if you can do it, is to have display tables with wheels. They are not cheap. I don't suggest you buy

one unless you have a lot of uses for such a thing. Most of us have the standard folding table and those aren't cheap either. But here's another way of looking at it: most tables don't come with wheels but a lot of desks do. If you have a desk with wheels, perhaps use that as one of your outdoor display tables. Another option is to get some casters from a home store and place them temporarily on the legs of your table. If you have the standard 6-foot folding table, the legs look as though they are sealed at the bottom. This is actually just a gasket that can be removed. They are there to protect your floor from scratching, so don't lose the gaskets. When you remove the gaskets, you'll find the leg is hollow. The insert able casters will work nicely as a temporary fix to be

able to roll your table in or out of the weather. It also
reduces the amount of lifting and carrying needed.

Take a look at your table(s) to
ensure you get the type of caster
you need. There's a caster for all
kinds of scenarios so if you don't
have a hollow leg table, try a
different type of caster. If you
need help try explaining what
you're trying to do to the manager
at the store to see what solutions they might have.

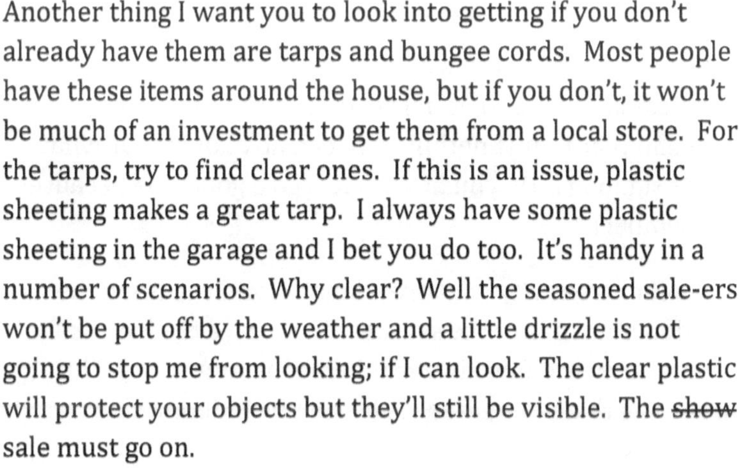

Another thing I want you to look into getting if you don't
already have them are tarps and bungee cords. Most people
have these items around the house, but if you don't, it won't
be much of an investment to get them from a local store. For
the tarps, try to find clear ones. If this is an issue, plastic
sheeting makes a great tarp. I always have some plastic
sheeting in the garage and I bet you do too. It's handy in a
number of scenarios. Why clear? Well the seasoned sale-ers
won't be put off by the weather and a little drizzle is not
going to stop me from looking; if I can look. The clear plastic
will protect your objects but they'll still be visible. The ~~show~~
sale must go on.

If you don't have a solid supply of bungee cords, make sure to
get some. While I want you to have as little overhead costs as
possible, these items will never go to waste so spend a little
now and use it forever. The bungees you'll use for several
things at the sale. In particular, should you have to use the
plastic to cover your tables, you'll use the bungees to secure
the plastic to the table. If you do decide to get a canopy, the
bungees can provide a bit of extra security in the tie down. If
you want to display something a bit special at your sale or if

you want to hang a sign temporarily, a bungee through the manual handle on your garage door can help and not leave a mark. Have a bunch of shovels and spades or other garden equipment with a handle? To prevent them falling down every five minutes, use the bungee to keep them all together or secure them to a sturdier surface. If you have larger pieces of furniture that you've got outside, a bit of plastic or tarp and a bungee can keep it high and dry. Also consider putting furniture actually ON the tarp instead of just a tarp over the furniture. This will help keep it clean and show sale-ers that it's quality and taken care of.

BRING THE PARTY INDOORS

All the preparation in the world can't protect you from the unpredictable. Sometimes a little drizzle can turn into a deluge and there's just nothing you can do about it. Or what if it isn't summer? Do you have to forego a good sale because it's December?

With a bit of creativity and street smarts, you can bring the sale indoors no matter the season. You'll have to plan wisely, of course, and carefully always thinking of your safety. But who's to say that your garage sale can't be indoors?

IN THE GARAGE (& LIVING ROOM & KITCHEN) SALE

Typically, an indoor sale would constitute a moving or estate sale. But what law says that has to be the case? Why not have an indoor garage sale? Garage sales shouldn't be limited to being outside. With climate change or just season change, you'll want to have more options than just a driveway to display your stuff.

But what would an indoor sale mean? A bunch of strangers going through your house? Is it safe? Well you'll have to plan wisely. Certain rooms and certain items will need to be secured. Estate sales block off certain areas of the house where they don't want people going in. Moving sales as well keep everyone to a certain area of the house where all the stuff for sale is available. It will take some extra effort on your part, but it can be very effective.

If you're not crazy about the idea of having people in your house, I understand completely. I'm not very comfortable with strangers in my house. By the same token, I'm really not crazy about going to stranger's houses. As a Sale-er I've been to a lot of these indoor/outdoor sales and I'm never quite comfortable going into a stranger's house. Example, over the summer a neighbor was having a garage/moving sale. He'd been out of work for a long time and his parents passed so he wanted to leave the state. He sat in a chair outside his garage and told me the tale. The garage items available weren't exactly treasures. He did have some tools but then said they weren't for sale so I couldn't really see a reason for me to stay. I was disappointed because he was very nice and I wanted to help. He then said he had a living room set in the house. As I was looking for furniture at the time, I thought I'd check it out. I asked if it was alright for me to take a look and he said sure. I thought he would show me in, but he sat there talking to other customers, which of course makes sense. I was on my own going through his house. I was very uncomfortable. It was a nice living room set. Still, I didn't really go in and take a look because I was extremely uncomfortable being there without him,

So, while you may be uncomfortable, be aware that your Sale-ers may be uncomfortable as well. If you relax, so will they. Have friends over for the day, especially important if you live alone, to help you with the sale. This will make you feel more comfortable and ease the burden of having to keep your eyes on everything and everyone. If you're so inclined, maybe serve cookies and coffee and cocoa. This makes it feel more like just having the neighbors over.

Let's talk about personal safety for a moment. Of course, you always want to protect yourself. You'll weigh your comfortability against the risks you take as you do with everything in your life. But I do want to point out that burglars and rapists and serial killers don't tend to frequent garage sales, indoor or out. They're typically pretty stupid. I recently saw on the news a couple of burglars trying to break in to a house with a ring camera recording the whole thing. The ring doorbell isn't very discreet. These idiots saw the camera and continued kicking the door trying to get in. It's broad daylight, the camera has got a perfect picture of them. But they just keep kicking. The only thing that made them stop was the owner speaking through the camera's speaker, "get away from my door". Then they took off like their hair was on fire. Stupid. Well, hey, they made the news.

My point is, obviously be careful, but not afraid. Most people are good. Everyone has their drama but generally people are decent and being afraid of them is a mistake. You could miss out on some amazing folks and opportunities because you're afraid of letting someone in.

If you just can't see yourself having strangers in your home, there's another option. Consider getting together with some of your neighbors and having an indoor garage sale at your local synagogue or church. Call it a rummage sale. Give a portion of the proceeds to the church or pay them for the use of their facilities.

Another way forward without strangers at your house is a sale at a storage facility. So many of us have storage rentals now. Why? If you can't have it in your house, why do you have it? A rant for another time. Clean out that storage rental and bank that money you're spending each month. To do this properly, you'll need to inform the facility that you're having people come by. It's wise to set some strict time guidelines as well. Maybe set appointment times as you won't want to sit at the storage facility all day. Make it an "invitation only" event. This will give it an exclusivity that is enticing to sale-ers.

Using a facility is a nice way to do your sale without having strangers in your home. You will have to pay a facility something, which will cut into your profits. In some cases, the facility will be cost-prohibitive. If that's the case you have two options, first, and I recommend this, find another facility. Second, get the neighbors to join you. Getting the neighbors to join you no matter the facility is a smart move. More neighbors mean more Sale-ers. Sale-ers love to go to multi-family sales. More cool junk to buy!

Other options for facilities include, town halls, park districts, libraries, community organizations, VFWs and one that I bet you never thought of, real estate agencies. Real estate agencies would love to help you and your neighbors. Of course, if they get to know you, you're more likely to give them a listing or a lead on a listing. This helps them and helps you. They may or may not have the facilities to help you with your sale, but they do have listings or know of listings for empty storefronts which would be a fantastic pop-up garage sale facility. This option would almost certainly require you to get your neighbors involved. If you simply can't get everyone organized, a booth at the swap meet or flea market is a very good option as well.

Don't let the weather or the season deter you from having a fantastic sale. An "off-season" sale is a great way to get rid of the junk. As an avid Sale-er I love these sales. It's so sad when the weather turns and the sales stop. Why should they? We all still have junk to get rid of and plenty of it. Think outside the box and with a little planning, you'll have the sale of the year.

CHAPTER 8. PLANNING THE LAYOUT

Yes, PLANNING the layout. The layout is one of the most critical steps in your sale planning. The way your "merchandise" (for lack of a better word) is displayed is one of the many things that can make or break your sale.

Sale-ers how many times have you decided whether or not to stop at a sale based on a drive-by? I actually don't recommend judging whether or not to stop by driving by. I do it, too; but it's not a good idea. You could miss a lot with a snap judgement and a snap judgement is all you have time for if you're just driving by. It's a difficult decision when you have a list of 10 sales to you want to visit. How do you figure out the sales that are a waste of time and get to the sales that have the good stuff? If you're wasting time, you could miss out on the find of the century at another sale. So, we do the drive by and if it looks promising we stop. If it doesn't, we don't. But I'm certain I've missed out on some great buys because I didn't think the sale was worth the time based on a glance from my car window.

Sellers, focus on your layout so your sale-ers are compelled to stop and look. Your layout is going to get the attention of the drive-by traffic in addition to your ad driven traffic. If it doesn't look good from the street, you'll be missing out on sales.

BUSINESS IN THE FRONT, PARTY IN THE BACK

So how do we go about the layout? What should go where?
Well let's return to our inventory. What are your star items?
What are your BIG items. Not the big-ticket items, but the big
stars that are going to attract people. I'm referring to the
furniture, bicycles, appliances. The things that catch the eye,
but are hard to walk away with. These are the things that
should go nearest the street. Smaller items that have a lot of
eye appeal should remain in the garage. Electronics, higher
priced items, collectibles, etc. should stay in the garage due to
the theft risk. iPads, cell phones, laptops, baseball card
collections, these kinds of items can walk. It's very unlikely
but you never know and while you may want to get rid of it,
you don't necessarily want it to disappear. Keep these items
close and perhaps make a sign or series of signs advertising
them near the end of your drive.

DIRECTING TRAFFIC

Consider how you want your sale-ers to discover your items.
Sellers have a lot of power in this regard. Consider how you
want them to negotiate the sale itself. Consider where you
want them to start and end. Place the items in an order that
makes sense. Having a table with kid's roller skates and a
pillow case, doesn't make sense. Sale-ers like to dig for
treasure but not that hard. Put your items in an order that
makes the most sense. Place like items with like items. Tools
to the right, housewares to the left, etc. Boxes of items are
ok, but be careful of the kind of items placed in the box.
Small items are problematic in a big box. Keep top-of-mind
the items you have and access to them. Don't assume that all
sale-ers will dig through the box. Toys are good for boxes
because kids will dig through a dumpster of elephant dung to
get a good toy. Think about access and think about your star

items and turn your garage/driveway into a department store.

You may want to take a picture of your space and then sketch out where you want things to go. Be sure to leave clear aisles for people to walk down unencumbered. Not only walk, either; be sure to leave enough room for those with special needs like wheelchairs. Try to leave at least 36 inches between your "aisles". Many times, people with access issues often feel left out of activities like garage sale-ing. Make sure your sale is welcome to all. Planning like this probably seems like overkill, but you're planning like this to show off your items in the best light. Remember, you'll be placing ads on apps and other areas that will require pictures. The Sale-ers see these pictures, probably on their phones, and say, "ooh, is that a...." Items placed randomly on tables isn't exactly screaming, "Gotta go to that sale!"

To give you a better idea of what I mean by sketching out your layout, I've created a kind of blueprint image of the layout for my sales. It's nothing more than a bunch of squares and rectangles. You can easily do it on your computer with a word processing program. Or you can do it with pad, pen and ruler. If you want to use the image that I've created, I've included the components at the end of the book. You can cut them out or copy and paste to create your ideal layout.

My Garage Sale Layout

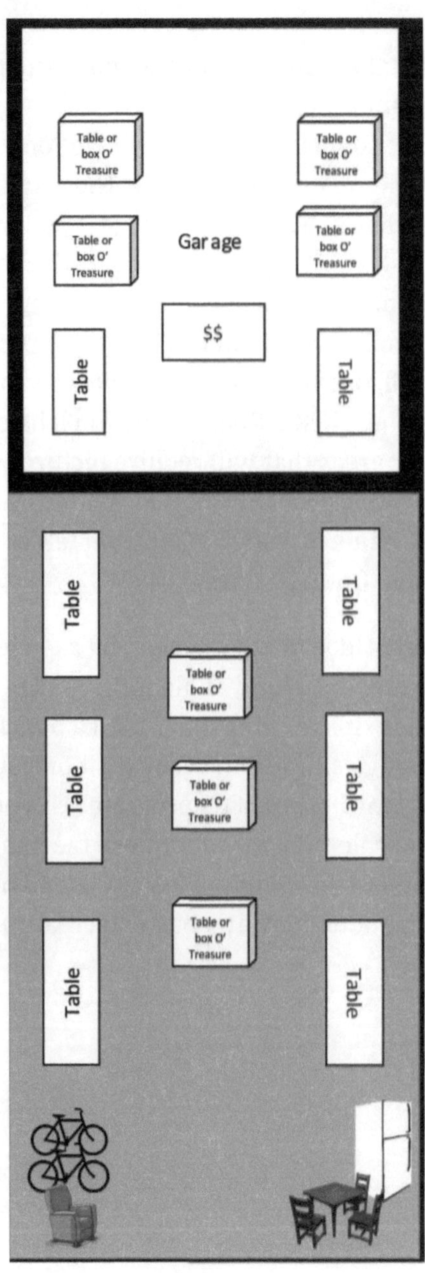

KIDDIELAND

Consider getting the kids out of the way. Sale-ers often bring the family along and the kids are the first to get bored. If they make themselves annoying enough, you could lose a sale or a number of sales. Kids are great but not when you want to go sale-ing. I've left sales where the kids were just too much. I've left stores for the same reason. Since you can't ask people to leave their kids at home, perhaps have a section just for them. I went to a sale once, probably about three years ago now, that had a bouncy house for the kids. I thought it was a brilliant move. The kids not only were entertained but they didn't want to leave so the parents stayed longer than they would and bought more than they would. A bouncy house probably isn't in the cards for most of us. Also, there's an insurance risk that I wouldn't have taken. However, if you have a bunch of toys in your sale, move these toys to the center of your lawn. Maybe even section off the area and place a sign saying, "KIDS ONLY". It cannot be out of sight of the parents but should be far enough away to give mom and dad a breather. The kids will play and the parents can shop. If you're concerned about the toys, don't be. To be honest, unless you've got some very cool toys in immaculate condition, they don't sell that well. In fact, you may want to give most of the toys away to the kids to get rid of them. Of course, providing the parents made a purchase.

PUTTING IT ALL TOGETHER

Okay we've got all the pieces, now it's time to put them together. I highly recommend doing a dry run on the set up and layout. Call it a dress rehearsal. At this point of the book, I would assume that you have your inventory, signs, tables and layout all ready to go. It's now time to set up the garage and driveway with all your items. You may get some Sale-ers passing by asking if you're open. You can play these one of two ways, first, you can tell them you're not open and they will need to come back and give them the time and date of the actual sale. This isn't as negative as it might appear. You can build anticipation with this method. "I'm sorry, no, not open just yet. I'm just getting everything together so I'm ready to go on (date). You certainly can look around but I'd feel bad about selling anything early because there's a lot of people coming for certain things." Of course, this is all nonsense, but the sale-er doesn't know that and if they have some interest in an item or two, the idea that that item might go to someone else if they don't act quickly will increase their interest exponentially. The second option is to say, "no, I'm not open, I'm just getting everything ready. But feel free to look around." If you're lucky, you may get a sale. Early money is nothing to sneer at.

Once you have everything set up, step back and take a look. Observe things with a critical eye and ask yourself are things where they should be? If you were a Sale-er, would you stop to take a look? Is this the best layout for the space? Move things around until you get it right. At this point you should also start pricing things in the method you've chosen. Once you have it the way you want it, step back again and take a picture of the entire layout. Next take picture of each of the tables and any of the items you want to call out as your "stars". Take plenty of pictures. Preferably at noonish or the brightest part of the day so you have plenty of light without using the flash. Of these pictures, select the best and use these pictures in your digital advertising. If you have a printer and are so inclined, you might even use them in your print advertising. Paste a copy of the picture(s) to your lawn signage. It will be difficult for people to see at a distance, but it will be an attention getter which is critical, particularly when you're in high g-sale season and there's an ad on every corner.

Once this is done, you're ready for show time, Congratulations!

Lightly re-pack the items for sale and place everything back in the garage. You may lose your parking place for a while, but if everything is already in the garage, the set-up will be that much easier.   Since we've done this dress rehearsal, your day of set-up will be incredibly fast and easy. See, I told you a little planning would pay off in a big way.

Chapter 9. Permits, Licenses and Fees, Oh My!

It's kind of amazing how many folks have their hand out when you're attempting to make an extra buck or two. Truly it's like they smell blood in the water or something because someone will always be there telling you what you can or cannot do unless you give them some money. Give them some money and you can run the hunger games out of your garage and there wouldn't be an issue.

When possible, the permit process should be undertaken as early in the planning as you can manage. Generally, in my neighborhood, they turn a blind eye to anyone having a sale without a permit. Generally. One of the people that works in our township office lives on my street. She's totally cool though and wouldn't report on you. But frankly, I find that life is a lot easier if you just let them pick your pocket for the permit. Ooops, accidental alliteration. I stay on the right side of everyone concerned and pay the fee. Why? Well, first off, the person that works at the office is totally cool, and I wouldn't take advantage like that. Second, you may get away with it 99 out of 100 times. But time number 100 is going to be a real drag and cause you all sorts of unnecessary drama. Finally, typically the fee for the permit isn't cost prohibitive but the cost for not getting the permit will be.

This chapter is all about keeping garage sale-ing safe and legal. I'm going to attempt to answer how one goes about finding out what the rules are regarding neighborhood sales? What to do if the costs are too high? What to do if you "forget" to get the permit? What the consequences might be if you decide to forego the permit process.

DO I NEED A PERMIT?

As I've mentioned before, my neighborhood puts on a neighborhood sale once per year. The announcement of the sale comes in a newsletter format which is conveniently on the backside of the water bill. It's a smart way of communicating it but still people don't read it. When the announcement comes out, they make it a point to say "we are waiving the permit fees for this event". Now if people did read the announcement, they really couldn't be under any doubt that permits are required for sales held outside of the event. But people don't read the announcements, and even if they did, they might not have made that connection. So, all summer and into the fall, there are sales without permits. I asked some of them if they had a permit and if they said no, I asked if they were concerned that they might get a violation notice. They weren't concerned in the least. I have not heard of anyone getting a ticket for not having the license.

So, what's the big deal? Why should you bother? As I said before, you can get away with it 99 out of 100 times, it's number 100 that's the problem. In my village, they are clear about the rules and cost of the permit, and consequences of non-compliance. The "Penalty" sections state that the fine is $25 but no more than $500. The fee for the permit is $2. Frankly, I don't see an issue with getting a permit. Is it annoying? You bet. If you like to live on the edge, chances are you'll be fine. But if others are paying for permits and you aren't, get ready for that to come back and bite you. I think the wisest move is to stay on the right side of the authorities at all times.

HOW DO I FIND OUT IF I NEED A PERMIT?

The easiest way to find out if your neighborhood requires a permit is to ask your town/village hall. If you don't get a definitive answer there, you can ask your local police department, but first and foremost, check the internet for your village ordinances. If it will be anywhere, it will be there. Here's what my village's ordinance looks like:

- ## GARAGE SALES
- ## § 115.045 - DEFINITIONS.

For the purpose of this subchapter, the following definitions shall apply unless the context clearly indicates or requires a different meaning.

DWELLING, BUILDING, STRUCTURE FOR PURPOSES OF THIS SUBCHAPTER. A place of human habitation for residential purposes as defined in the zoning code.

GARAGE SALE. All general sales, open to the public, conducted from or on a premise or premises located in a residentially zoned district, as defined by the zoning code, for the purpose of disposing of personal property including, but not limited to, all sales entitled "garage," "lawn," "yard," "attic," "porch," "room," "backyard," "patio," "flea market," "rummage sale," or any similar casual sale of tangible personal property which is advertised by means whereby the public at large is or can be aware of the sale.

PERSONAL PROPERTY. Property which is owned, utilized and maintained by an individual or members of his or her residence and acquired in the normal course of living in or maintaining a residence. It does not include merchandise which was purchased for resale or obtained on consignment or warehouse merchandise.

(Ord. 92-18, passed 9-22-92)

- ## § 115.046 - LICENSE REQUIRED; FEE.

It shall be unlawful for any person to conduct a garage sale in the village without first filing with the Village Clerk the information hereinafter specified and obtaining from such Clerk a license to do so, to be known as a "Garage Sale License." The fee for such license shall be $2.

115.999 - PENALTY.

(A)

Any person, firm, or corporation who violates any provision of this chapter for which another penalty is not specifically provided shall, upon conviction, be subject to a fine of not less than $25, nor more than $500, and the costs of prosecution. A separate offense shall be deemed committed upon each day during which a violation occurs or continues.

(B)

Any person convicted of a subsequent violation of §§through_ within 24 months of a previous offense shall be fined a minimum of not less than $100 nor more than $500, and the cost of prosecution. A separate offense shall be deemed committed upon each day during which such violation occurs or continues.

As you see, the penalties for non-compliance can be pretty severe. Again, I've never heard of anyone being prosecuted, but I don't want to be the first so I'll pay the $2. Find out for sure. Check the internet, check with your town government, check with the police department. Document your search for answers. If you're searching online, use garage sale as it's the most common name for home good sales. If you use the search term "yard sale" you may not get the desired results. I had a bit of a challenge finding the rules. The table of contents didn't list garage sale law or anything. I took a chance and used the site's search engine and it pulled it right up. If you don't get anywhere online or with your local government or the police department, just be sure you document who you spoke to and when. This shouldn't be necessary but if you have it all documented and something goes awry, you'll be able to fight back.

I LIVE IN A BIG CITY, I DON'T NEED A PERMIT

Before I moved to the suburbs, I lived in my beloved Chicago. I grew up there. It's an amazing place. Here is the ordinance regarding sales in Chicago:

Garage, Yard & Apartment Sale Permit, Sanitation

The Permit Process

Chicagoans planning to hold garage, yard and apartment sales can obtain their required permits at any of the city's **50 Aldermen ward offices**. Locations of these ward offices can also be obtained by calling the city's 311 non-emergency number.

As of October 1, 1996, the Chicago City Council passed an ordinance requiring such permits to guard against seemingly perpetual yard sales that actually were serving as unlicensed retail operations in residential neighborhoods. The ordinance limits each household to two per calendar year, unless a third sale is needed because the applicant is moving permanently from their residence.

All such sales are limited in duration to three consecutive days between 9:00 a.m. and sunset. In case of rain, the sale can be held during the next three days after the permit period, but is still limited to three total days. If more than one household is joining in a single sale, each household needs its own permit even if the sale is at the address of only one participating household.

The ordinance specifically prohibits advertising these sales with signs posted anywhere except on the property where the sale is taking place. Violators face fines ranging from $50 to $500 with each day representing a separate offense.

Charitable organizations, churches and schools are exempt from the ordinance. To get your permit, complete the attached application form and mail it at least two weeks prior to the starting date.

There is no fee for obtaining these permits.

The good news is, there's no fee for the permits. I think admittedly the city would be the first to say they wouldn't use resources to deal with non-permit holding garage sales. My point is, don't take for granted that you don't need a permit. To be honest, when I lived in the city and wanted to have a sale, I never got a permit. If you're living in a big city, chances are G-Sale permits aren't high on the city's agenda, but, one thing I want you to consider for those of you in a large city planning a sale without a permit. Should you follow the guidelines in this book, you are going to have a terrific turnout. If you find you have crowds of people and cars trying to get to your sale, much like that sale I told you about in the beginning of this book, you may attract law enforcement attention. Crowds of people and cars can be an issue. If someone can't get to their house because of your garage sale, you can bet the police will be called. If they are called, the first thing they will ask you about is a permit. If you don't have one, you will get ticketed.

WHAT IF THE COST FOR THE PERMIT IS TOO HIGH?

Well, for all the work that goes into organizing and preparing for your garage sale, if you ask me, any amount paid for a permit is too much. I think if they want a portion of the profits of your sale, they should help with the workload. But since we're not in kimmyland, let's deal with reality. The costs of these permits run the gambit. In my research I didn't really find an average price. Palm Springs seems to be the highest at $20. Long Beach is $17 also pretty high. The majority seems to run about $5 or less. If you find that the cost of the permit is too high in your municipality, there are some options:

1) you can partner with your neighbors. Now a word about that, in many of the ordinances I've read it addresses the idea of partnering with neighbors. They typically state that each neighbor is required to pay for the permit even if the sale is held at one location. So, if you opt for this plan, you may not be able to split the cost of the permit.

2) See if there is a day where the fees for the permit are waived. As I've mentioned, my neighborhood waives the permit requirement for their garage sale weekend. Many townships and villages do the same. If your local government does this and you can accommodate the change in dates, you might come out ahead.

3) if the cost of the permit is prohibitive and you can't find a workaround, consider an alternative venue. We talked earlier about the flea market. Now the cost of a flea market booth is probably in excess of the cost of a permit, but if the cost of the permit is high and you don't think you will get a return on that investment, the flea market might be a viable alternative. If you have to pay a fee at the very least the flea market has dedicated, definite traffic. Now they have slow days of course and there's no guarantee that what you get will be what the patrons you are looking for, but if the stars align, so to speak, it could work toward your advantage.

Additionally, with the flea market, you can partner with neighbors and split the costs without penalty so in the end it might be the best option to combat unreasonable fees.

BETTER TO ASK FOR FORGIVENESS THAN PERMISSION

I've mentioned before that I think it's better to stay on the right side of those in power. But it's entirely possible, with all the planning that goes into having a garage sale, that the permit process gets missed. Having said that, I don't think it's wise to play dumb. If your neighborhood requires getting a permit, get the permit. If you do forget, try to make it right. If you get caught and they ticket you, try to be honest and contrite about the error. There are a lot of reasons for permit requirements. It's not just about picking your pocket, although it can feel like that's all there is to it.

There is a house about a block from me that has a clothing sale almost every day of the summer. The village finally shut it down, but it was really ridiculous and pretty obvious that they were running a business. Every day they pulled open their garage door, put up a blue tarp to extend their "shop" and pulled out all the clothes and shoes you could imagine. There were quinceanera dresses and coats and shoes. It was like going to a street sale in Tijuana. Many of the so-called sales in my neighborhood feature clothes, which I just abhor, but this was excessive. They must have had a lot of complaints because this past year they were out only briefly. I later found out that the village fined them for running a business without a license. The point is, if a permit is required for the garage sale, in theory, stories like this one won't happen.

As I've mentioned, I don't think an unlicensed garage sale is a high priority for local government. But I do think that if everyone is paying for the permit and you do not, you're asking for a fight. No one likes the idea of paying for these things. I hate it. I had to pay for a permit to have my roof done. The idea was that the village would "inspect" the work. But what if I hadn't gotten the permit? Well I would have gotten a ticket for sure, but more than that, if something had happened I could lose a lot. They never came by for the inspection, by the way, but sometimes it's just not worth the risk. So, I give the village their "cut" as I refer to it.

It's possible, though really unlikely, that you could be denied for a permit. So "forgetting" this step is a real risk. I've discovered that the reasons for denying a permit are typically logistical. Example: my village has a 4th of July parade. It's such a nuisance, it's impossible to get out of my neighborhood as they have the major arteries blocked off. The 4th seems like a really good day to do a garage sale, but if no one can get to my sale, well, not so good. The village considers this and won't issue permits for Independence Day. Think wisely and if you do forget or legitimately miss the permit process, hopefully you won't suffer any consequences. Ask for forgiveness if necessary, but ask for permission when possible.

CHAPTER 10. OK SALE-ERS, LET'S GET SALE-ING

Hey Sale-ers, is there anything better than a day of garage sale-ing? Well, maybe one or two things, but you have to admit digging for fun junk at insane prices is a stellar day out. You know I wrote this book primarily with the Sale-er in mind. I know I've spent a lot of time on how to put on the best sale possible, but that's because I'm hoping I can help up the quality of the sales out there. I don't know what you've encountered but my sale-ing has been pretty dismal as of late. In any season you can really only hope for a couple of above standard sales, but lately I've been lucky to find one really good one. So hence the conception of the G-Sale bible. A book where Sellers and Sale-ers can put on and locate the best possible sale.

Let's focus on finding that perfect sale. How do you start? Well, first, much like a seller, what's your motivation? Are you looking for something in particular or are you just looking? Do you want to keep to your neighborhood or are you up for an adventure? How are your negotiating skills? Are you willing to pay a bit more for the right item or are you a "stick to your guns" sale-er? Well, this chapter is all about us and the strategies a good sale-er has to find and get the good stuff!

WHAT'S YOUR MOTIVATION?

If a seller has to determine their motivation, it's even more important for a sale-er. Why? Because if you know what you want and what you're willing to do to get it, the world is your oyster. As with life, the same with sale-ing. If you know what you're looking for and what you're willing to pay for it, you're halfway to getting it. The problem is we sale-ers usually go out without a clear direction. If we happen upon a sale, we browse and if something looks good we get it. As your fellow sale-er, I can tell you I'm particularly guilty of this kind of sale-ing. It's fun, directionless, time-wasting, but really fun. There's no right or wrong way to answer the question, "What's your motivation?" But it's a good idea to know the answer before you go out. If you go with the "just browsing" method, you should do so deliberately. If you know what you want and are out to get it, equally, you don't waste time.

PLAN ACCORDINGLY

Think about what you want to accomplish and then plan accordingly. If you're just out to enjoy the day, terrific, but don't take a lot of cash. You'll burn through it and then feel guilty. Take $20 or $30 and no more. If there's something you really want, you can always go get more cash. In a previous chapter I mentioned that leaving to go get cash gives a sale-er time to think. This may not be great for the seller but it is beneficial for a sale-er. If you have to go get more cash for this item, is it really worth it?

If you're on the lookout for something special, make sure you have a plan in place. Target the sales most likely to have what you're looking for. Sometimes this is easier said than done, I KNOW. Plot out the sales you want to hit. If what you want isn't at the sale you're at, move on. That's the hard part for me. I'll be at a sale and know they don't have what I'm looking for but I spend 20 minutes there anyway just browsing at what they do have or I'll be running my mouth with the seller. There's nothing particularly wrong with this if you're not looking for something specific, but if you are, this can hold you back from your goal. I can't tell you how many times I've missed out on something because I was wasting time at other sales.

STICK CLOSE TO HOME OR JACK KEROUAC IT

There's a logic to sticking close to home when garage sale-ing. If you're trying to save money on an object and have to drive 40 miles to get it, well maybe you just head to the "store that shall not be named" and pay the extra. In addition, visiting sales that are close to home keeps your money in the neighborhood and the planet will thank you for walking instead of driving. However, sticking close to home has its disadvantages. It's best suited to you if your motivation is just to enjoy the day going to random sales. If you're on a mission to find that something special, staying in your neighborhood limits your opportunities.

If you're up for an adventure, you can really have a lot of fun sale-ing and exploring a new neighborhood. Planning is key to a day like this. Have a plan and have a back-up plan. Make a list of all the sales available in the area you are going to and head directly there. If you divert because you saw a sale you have to stop at, by all means, but know that this will put a crimp in the schedule and could derail it altogether.

Once you're in the neighborhood you've chosen, how are the sales? Sometimes you find that the grass isn't actually greener at all and maybe you should have stuck closer to home. But that doesn't mean all the sales are lame. It just means that you'll want to shorten the amount of time spent at these sales unless you find a good one. Visit all the sales you planned to, limiting the amount of time spent at the weak ones. Now here's where plan B comes in. If you find the neighborhood you've visited just isn't what you'd hoped, have a plan B for another neighborhood of sales. Preferably one nearby the lame sale neighborhood. With any luck, you should find at least one good sale. If not, maybe it's just one of those days and at least you're out and about. Try to find a neighborhood with sales within walking distance of each other. Park the car and walk around the neighborhood. Your Fitbit will thank you.

WHAT KIND OF NEIGHBORHOOD IS THIS?

Where I live we have certain neighborhoods that are upper-middle class and some that are very upper class. We refer to these areas as the "Northshore". They tend to encompass a bit more than just the actual North shore, but it's more of a mindset than an actual location. These are the million-dollar homes, "car costs more than my house" kind of homes. I'm sure you have a few "Northshore" neighborhoods where you live. These neighborhoods have garage sales and, on the surface, it seems like a spectacular place to go sale-ing. They are generally pretty neat sales. As you can imagine, the stuff they have for sale is higher-end, mostly. The only problem with sale-ing in these neighborhoods is that the sellers really don't have the same perspective on money that most people have.

I went to a sale in Northbrook, a suburb of Chicago-very Northshore, this sale didn't have much of anything I was interested in. They did have a little red tool box. (wouldn't you know it would be something to do with tools) It was just what you'd think of when I say little red tool box. Metal, rusty, black handle, maybe holds a hammer and a socket wrench. I was actually only half-interested, to be fair. I wanted a tool box but I like something more modern and can carry a lot. Still, tool boxes in my house never go to waste and I thought I could keep some of the basic household tools

in it. I asked the woman running the sale how much she
wanted for it. Wait for it....$20. You know, I'm an expressive
type of personality and it's hard for me to keep a poker face.
I really tried, but I was stunned. This thing had to be as old
as I was and it's just a little tool box. I didn't say anything
and politely put the tool box down. She must have seen
through my bad poker face because she said, "It's an
antique". Folks, it was hardly going to make the Roadshow.
It's old, but honestly, all of our dads have one of these
toolboxes in the shed. I suppose I could have seen $5, but
$20? And to be honest, I wouldn't have paid the $5. It wasn't
in the best of condition and it's not going to hold a lot. I
thought to myself, "yeah, Northshore".

I think if you have money, you think everyone has money or
maybe it's just that you don't have a sense of the real value of
money. It's kind of like the politician not knowing the price
of milk. It's just not really in their wheelhouse. They've lost
touch, if they ever had touch, with the real value of things
and what it means to a working-class individual. The woman
was selling a few things, but it was to other Northshore folks.

So why have I told you this story? Well when you're planning
an adventure day garage sale-ing, it can be very tempting to
go to the upper-class part of town. It's actually pretty smart.
You may get a great deal. But keep in mind that these people
pay $15K for their living room furniture. It's not likely their
going to sell you their old $10K set for $100. A good deal to
you and a good deal to them are probably two completely
different things. Be prepared to fork out a lot more cash, but
if you're in the market for higher end things, these
neighborhoods can be a gold mine. If you're in the "I'll give
you a dollar for it" camp like most of us, maybe these aren't
the sales for you. I actually don't go to these sales anymore.

If I happen to be there and have time to kill, I'll stop and look, but I won't really even bother trying to get anything. It's really not my style. I can appreciate higher end items, but I'm not going to buy them. I'm fairly Spartan with my home. With dogs everywhere, I just can't see spending a lot on anything. Even when I make my millions from this book.

I can't tell which is funnier, the fact that Neiman won't throw in the shipping or the 25% off if you use the coupon code "FRIENDME"

P.S. the shipping is more than I paid for my entire living room set.

You want HOW Much?

Ok sale-ers, how good are you at negotiations? Are you fair or do you low ball? Do you get a price in your mind and stick to it or will you pay a bit more? Are you a bit shy or fairly brazen? You'll be surprised at this, but I don't think there's a wrong answer here. So much depends on who you are and how you feel and think. If you're okay with paying $20 for the tool box, I'm not going to judge you. When it comes to negotiating deals, value is really in the "eye of the beholder". Some people aren't comfortable at all negotiating a better price and therefore will pay the price or walk away. There are no wrong answers but here I want to help you negotiate better, if possible.

PLAY FAIR OR NOT AT ALL

Do you recall earlier I told you the story of my sectional and the guy that wanted it delivered? That guy was a jerk. It's a terrible thing to say, but unfortunately true. I don't have a problem with low balling as long as it's within reason and honest. I try to be fair in all my dealings. There's just no reason to be nasty about these things. If this guy had said, I want it but I can't give anywhere close to what you're asking, I may or may not have responded favorably, but I would have respected the honesty. To come to my house, playing games about delivery and false promises to respond back. That's just dishonest and unfair.

If I see something I want, but I think the price is ridiculous, I may attempt to negotiate a better price. 9 times out of 10, I just give them my bottom-line price. It might be smarter to go lower and negotiate up to my bottom-line price. For me, I just want to be straight with people. I find that my bottom-line price is really low and to go lower still in an attempt to negotiate up to my bottom-line doesn't typically work for me. Most of the time they are like the "tool lady" and shrug me off as some low-baller. It's always a mistake to shrug off anyone making an offer, but people do.

There's another school of thought that they might take your low-ball offer. You may be willing to pay $100 but you offer $50 and they take the $50. I don't know how often this really works. It doesn't really fit my style. But that doesn't mean it's not a good strategy. If that strategy works for you, and doesn't piss off your seller, terrific. I think I'm a bit more risk adverse. You see, a strategy where you offer lower than you're willing to pay only works if you're willing to walk away from the deal if it goes sideways. If you're willing to pay $100 but offer $50 on an item that's priced at $200, more than likely you're going to get an annoyed seller. They could go into their rant about how much they paid, or they could just tell you to get lost. If you're okay with those consequences, then that might be the strategy for you. Additionally, you look like a jerk if you can clearly see the item is a high-end item that you'd pay $2K for in the store and you try to get it for $50. I personally consider a few factors when I'm determining a price to offer:

- Do I really want this item?
- What am I willing to pay for this item? What's my bottom-line price?
- Is my offer reasonable in relation to the item's worth?
- Is my offer reasonable against what the item is priced at?

I want to be reasonable to the seller when I make an offer. There are valid reasons for their pricing decisions and we as Sale-ers should recognize that. We don't have to agree with the price, but you shouldn't dismiss it out of hand. When I make the offer, I try to come as close the the seller's price as I can without breaking my bottom-line.

I've always wanted a Chair and a half. I love to read and something about a snuggly chair and a half, with or without an ottoman, and a good book and my dogs, just oozes comfort to me. I wasn't really looking. But I found the

perfect one. It even had an ottoman. It was brown which then matched the sectional. The fabric was really nice. I could tell from the picture how comfortable it was. One problem, the price, $350. I loved this chair, it was more than 50 miles away from me and I still wanted it. Here's the picture from the ad:

Given the price, I didn't make an offer on it. Folks there are a few things I will spend money on: 1) Dogs, 2) the house (although I will try to spend as little as possible) 3) I can't think of a third. I may be cheap. I think I'm just thrifty but I'm probably cheap. Still, if you're buying used furniture, it should be used price.

A month went by and the chair was still there. I don't like making low offers. I don't want a pissed off seller and honestly the rant about how much they paid for their crap just gives me a migraine. I decided that if it was still there in another week, I might make an offer. It was and I did. I was very cordial about it and apologized for the low offer. But the most I could pay was $100. This was my bottom-line price. I only offered that much because of the quality. I don't believe in paying a lot for used furniture.

The seller got back to me and assured me that she wasn't offended, which I was grateful for, and she then told me what she paid for it. I was understanding and advised that I couldn't pay more than the $100. She declined the offer. I replied, I understood and that the offer was still there if she changed her mind.

After that, I let it go. That's what I mean about being able to walk away. If you can't pay them what they're asking, you have to be willing to walk. I think it was about a month later, she reached out to me and asked me to consider, $150. I thanked her, but couldn't do more than $100. That $100 was my budget and I would not move off that number. That's another key thing we as sale-ers must do. We have to stick to our guns on price. That was the piece's value to me. That's what I was willing to pay. I would have preferred $50. It is just a chair/ottoman. But I want to be reasonable with the seller and come as close as I can to her price without breaking my budget. She sold it to me for $100. It was quite the adventure. I rented a truck from Home D and of course that was the first snow of the season. It got a little wet but I got it home.

I love that chair, this was two years ago now, my dogs destroyed the ottoman about a week after I got my chair home. Now do you see why I don't pay a lot for things? I was so upset. Totally ripped it up. They know I worship the ground they walk on because despite my yelling at them, they continued to try and tear it up. I tried to find a replacement, but it's no longer made. It doesn't matter now because we've changed colors in the room and it doesn't go any more. I've tried slip covers because I love that chair, but really it's more or less in need of a new home. I just can't let it go,.. yet.

The point of this story is that I find the best strategy is to be fair, honest, a bit tough, but always respectful. If this woman told me to jump in the lake, I would have had to understand. The hardest part for me is being able to walk if it doesn't go my way. No matter what strategy works best for you, I urge you to keep in mind, playing fair and being reasonable and respectful.

STICK TO YOUR GUNS

I wrote that I do some careful consideration before making an offer on anything. Pretty much my main consideration is what I will pay for anything vs. my need or desire for something. When it comes to buying, this is really what it comes down to. Now the problem is sticking to that figure, whatever it is. It can be a real challenge. I've stated already that you have to be willing to walk away if the price is too much. That's sometimes easier said than done. There are some items that are necessities and cannot be negotiated. You can shop for groceries where you want but the cost of them cannot be negotiated. However, you can walk away from one store that's charging $1.50 for a dozen eggs in favor of another store selling 24 for $.99.

When you're sale-ing and you find that one of a kind item, try to remember that it's really not one-of-a kind. When you look at this terrific thing, whatever it is, you have to detach your emotions from it. Fix a critical eye on it. Determine what you will pay based on your budget and what you feel it's worth. Once you fix that price, don't go past it. It can be a real challenge, but the alternative is you paying more than you really wanted and that always being a part of the story of that item.

It's a real challenge. If the item is popular, you risk losing it altogether. But you simply have to stick to your price and be willing to walk away. The good news is, if it is a popular item, chances are you can find another. But no matter what, you must stick to your guns.

Challenge yourself on your next sale-ing adventure. If you find something you like, but the price is a bit high, take a breath and think; What am I willing to pay? Is this my bottom-line price? Can I walk away from it if my offer isn't accepted?

FAINT HEART NEVER WON FAIR MAIDEN OR THAT REALLY COOL TOASTER OVEN

When I was a little girl, I was very shy. I loved my grandpa so much but I can remember feeling frightened to show him that love. One day, on our weekly trip to his house, my mother told me that I hurt his feelings when I didn't talk to grandpa. This upset me so much. It's one of my earliest memories. I couldn't have been more than three or four years old. I just couldn't bear the thought of hurting my grandpa's feelings. I spoke up after that and he fed me steak, and we were besties from there out.

Now I tell you this story, not because I want to share my mom's poor parenting skills or my budding co-dependency at age three. I'm sharing this story because if you're timid around strangers, while you can't help how you feel, you may be sending a message that you never intended. People don't really understand shyness. No one thinks they could be intimidating. In fact, most people think they are the least intimidating person in the world. But that's not true, is it?

I don't want to get into a psychological tirade here. I'm not qualified and this isn't that kind of book. I do want to impart that while going up to a stranger and telling them what you'll pay for their set of china can be intimidating, consider it from the seller's point of view. If you can, try to step into their shoes for just a moment. They see you, looking at the set of china, that they are desperate to sell. No one else is looking at it. They're secretly hoping you want it. They don't want to scare you away, so they hang back. Maybe they give you a broad smile but they don't say anything in case you change your mind or maybe they do say something like, "Nice, isn't it?" Back in your own shoes, now you're even more nervous because they want $50 for the set and you don't think it's worth $30. You want to pay $25, no more. It's a nice set but how often will you really use it? Still, offering them half the price they're asking, whew, that's scary. I mean what if they get mad?

My response to you is, what if they do? Here's the one thing maybe my mother should have said, you're not responsible for the seller's feelings. The worst thing they could say is "No". This is what the item is worth to you. If they want to sell it, you will buy it but for YOUR price. You have a voice and it deserves to be heard. So, what if they don't like it? So, what if they get mad? They mean nothing to your life. They don't pay your bills, as an old boss told me once upon a time. Your timidity doesn't get you or the seller anything. You don't get the china and they don't get a sale of the china. A word from you gets the ball rolling. Just a word.

Getting past shyness isn't easy. Take it a step at a time. Bring a friend if it helps. Once you master this, the whole world will open up. Just remember, you have a voice and it deserves to be heard.

The Meek may inherit the Earth but I'm getting that Cookware set

Are you on the opposite spectrum from shy? I am too. I can relate to those who are shy because I was timid and I still feel those feelings, I just don't let them stop me anymore. Every now and again those feelings trip me up and throw me off my game. I think this happened with the jerk that came for my sectional. He was somewhat intimidating and I wasn't prepared for that. I get that way when I'm selling in particular. Not so much when I'm buying though. If I'm in top form, I can almost go over the line and that's what this section is about.

Sometimes, when we're negotiating or just browsing, we might be a bit intimidating, which isn't the best way to get what you want. I think sellers, or anyone really, appreciate honest, direct but respectful encounters. I know I always want to demonstrate this, however, I'm not certain I always do.

For the more brazen among us, I propose the same exercise as with the less confident. Take a minute, put yourself in the seller's shoes. You want the china but you're not willing to pay more than $25. You walk right up to the seller and tell them, "Hi, listen, I'll give you $25 for the china right now, you want it?" Well, now back in the seller's shoes for the moment, they're in a bit of dilemma. They want the china gone, for sure, but they're not loving the offer or the way it was delivered. It's kind of intimidating and disrespectful. Why should I sell it for half the price? The seller begins to think. Who does this guy think he is telling me what he's going to pay? This seller is leaning toward declining the offer, even though it might be the only offer he gets, simply because of the delivery of that offer.

Your intention probably isn't to go all caveman on him. You want the china and you've got things to do. You don't want to futz around on negotiating. That's all you intended, but that's not how it was received.

When approaching the seller with an offer they may not like, it's important to recognize that they probably won't like the offer and show some empathy for their feelings without moving on your price. This is sweet skill if you can pull it off. Look again at it from their point of view. This item means something to them or they wouldn't have priced it so high. Understanding that is going to help you help them let go of the expectation that they're going to get $50 for a set of china in the 21st century. Asking them to tell you about the set will go a long way in building a rapport with the seller. You don't really want to know its history, neither would I, I told you people telling me how much they paid for their stuff just annoys me. But that's really a fault in my character. You know, people's stuff means something to them. I'm more on the Spartan end of the spectrum. This is based on my history and the fact that I don't put a lot of value in anything except living creatures. So, if I can get past that and hear them out, I do appreciate the history. But I still won't pay more than my price. Once you hear them tell you about the china, you have more information to work with on your offer. Perhaps they tell you, "Ugh, I've had that set since we got married. I never use it anymore (hello 21st century). I never really liked it anyway." Hmmm, maybe they priced at $50 because they thought it was worth that. Maybe you could offer $15? Or the seller could say, "Ugh, I hate to get rid of it. I can't believe I'm selling it. It's been passed down for generations. I just

don't have the space and none of my kids want it. It's so sad."
Hmmm, better stick with the offer of $25.

You're much more likely to get your desired result if you
respect the seller and appreciate their point of view. In the
end, the item is only worth what the market will bear. But if
the seller thinks otherwise, you're not going to change their
mind. Being the proverbial bull in a china shop is definitely
not going to work. Perhaps ask them if they would consider
an offer. Then make your offer politely, even apologetically. If
they refused and you really want it, ask the seller to take
your number, in case they change their mind. You have to be
prepared to walk if the price isn't right. There is always
another opportunity and nothing is really one-of-a-kind.

SALE-ING WITH FRIENDS

Well my beloved sellers and sale-ers, we're nearing the end
now and I want to make sure to remind you, whether or
selling or sale-ing, to invite at least one friend.

I was introduced to Sale-ing by my mother. We would go out
on a Saturday or Sunday and see what the world had to offer.
The best sales I ever had always had plenty of friends and
neighbors sitting in lawn chairs and drinking ice tea. We
might not have sold much but we had a great time. I
encourage you to invite someone who has never done a
garage sale. You know how much fun it is, share it with
someone who doesn't. If you don't have someone new to
share it with, consider getting back in touch with someone
you haven't seen in a while. It's a great activity with friends
even if you don't buy or sell a thing. And it's a great way to
reconnect. You may wonder why you haven't done it sooner

or you may remember why you haven't. Either way, it's just more fun with friends as is with much of everything in life.

Thank you so much for reading this book. I hope you found it helpful. More importantly I hope this book inspires some spectacular sales. Anything good? Share with me your finds or let me know how your sale went. I'm on Twitter: @FosterKimberly. Make sure you let me know where the good sales are at! I'll happily re-tweet. (unless there's something I want. JK)

PRICING TOOL

My Item	Google $	eBay $	Craigslist $	Apps $	My price
Ex:Air fryer	$42.98	$25.69	$30.00	$40.00	$15

Garage sale Layout tools

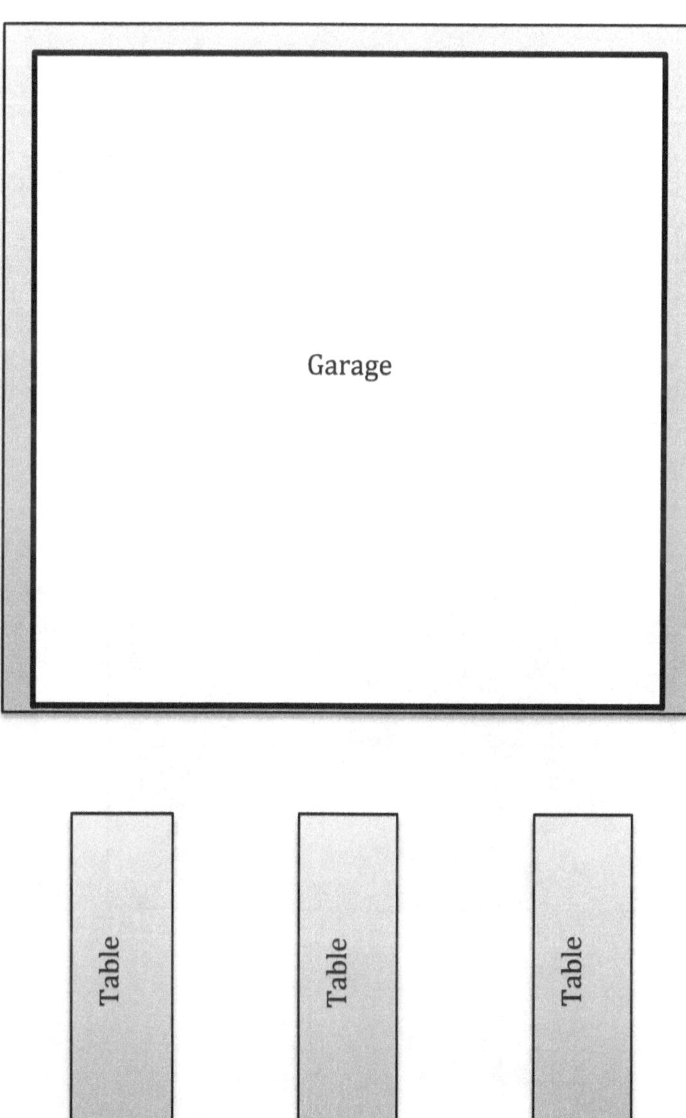

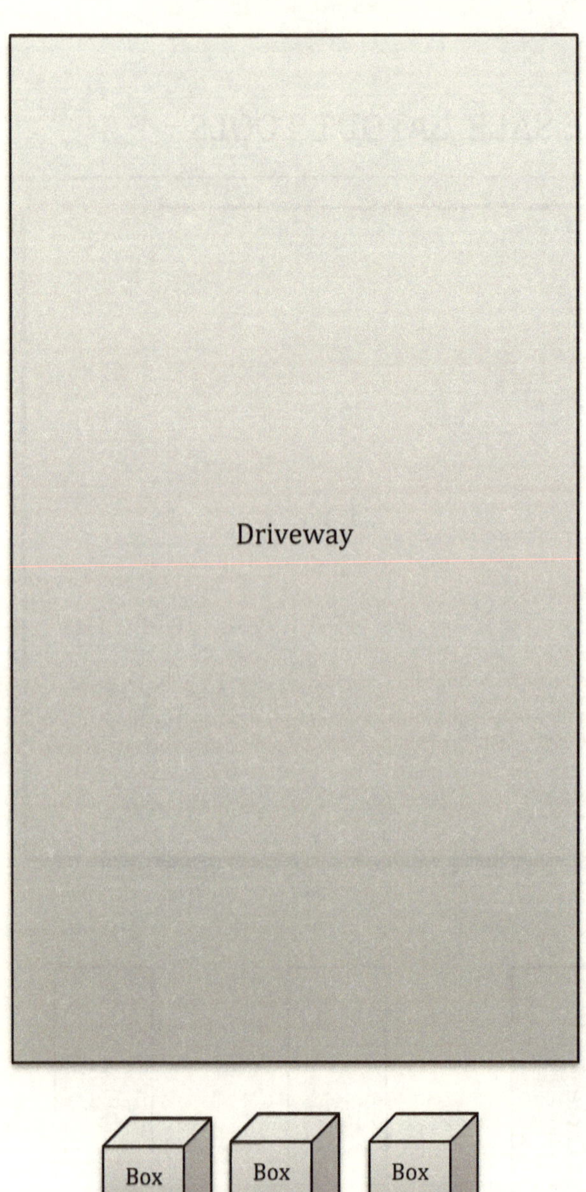
Driveway
Box
Box
Box

Bonus: How to Organize a Neighborhood Sale

A neighborhood sale can be a terrific idea and a logistical nightmare at the same time. Question: Do you have what it takes? If you have even a moment's hesitation, you are wise. Take it on only if you have a ton of energy and a keen understanding of people's foibles. This chapter is an abbreviated guide to help you get a neighborhood sale organized. There is a lot more that can be said. In fact, I could probably devote an entire book to the subject. But for the purposes of this book, I'm sharing with you the top-line considerations to keep in mind to give you a good idea of what is required.

First things first, get as much help as you can muster. You're going to need all the help you can get because there's a lot to do. Hopefully you have a small but reliable network of neighbors, if not, here's your chance to build it. Start out with inviting everyone over for an afternoon coffee/tea party. How? Perhaps print out a few invitation flyers and then go door-to-door. If you can find out where members of your local government live, be sure to invite them personally.

Once you've got everyone together, broach the idea of the sale. You could make an announcement, thanking everyone for coming and then share the idea. Initially, everyone will agree to the idea. Why shouldn't they? It's only when you outline the amount of work in planning that people will start to back out. Be prepared, have several "leaders" and back-ups. Start a "sign-up" sheet. Ask those signing up where they would like to provide their assistance, i.e., leadership, door-to-door, clean-up, etc.

Outline the next steps for everyone, but get their thoughts. Don't over-control the group. Listen patiently to even the dumb ideas. Get some pens and paper and maybe even a flip chart to write down everything. Brainstorm with the group as this will help with bonding as well as get some cool ideas. When you come to agreement on a basic plan, that concludes the first meeting of the organizing committee. Now let's talk about the next steps:

First, discuss timing for the next meeting. It's important that you set a date, time and location for meeting two with your neighbors. Get a time and date that the majority can agree on. You will not get everyone back a second time. Just be prepared for it by having more people than you need.

MEETING TWO:

Meeting two will be all about the checklist. You will need to have this checklist and present it to your neighbors. The checklist will be the next steps and must-haves for the sale to be successful. Allow the committee to add to or eliminate items off the list. Here's an initial checklist you can use as a guideline (Not set in stone, just a starting point):

- ❑ Local government approval/buy-in
- ❑ Agreed upon date
- ❑ Participating neighbors list
- ❑ Communication/advertisement
- ❑ Local business buy-in
- ❑ Larger purpose message/i.e. charity or neighborhood project
- ❑ After sale clean up

A lot is encompassed in this check list so let's start one at a time:

LOCAL GOVERNMENT APPROVAL AND BUY-IN

You will need the approval & assistance of your local government if you are to succeed. To be honest it, it's almost more important than getting the neighbor's initial buy in. Your local government can shut you down before you've even started, so this step cannot be skipped and must be the very next step after getting the neighbors to buy in.

If at all possible, invite members of the local government to your neighbor coffee party. I'm lucky in that I have a member of local government four doors down. If you can, try to find your town official's home and invite them personally. The earlier you know what to expect from the local officials, the easier your next steps will be.

Ask your group to have a committee devoted to dealing with the local government and the steps involved in getting approval for the sale. This subset of the larger group will be in charge of meeting with officials, presenting to town councils and getting the permit(s). In order for this committee to succeed, they will need to have as many details regarding the plans as possible. The committee will have to go back and forth to local officials as things change, but we want to limit that as much as humanly possible. So, let's talk details.

AGREED UPON DATE

The date of the sale is the first hurdle that you'll have to tackle. It's not going to be easy, and you'll have a lot of back and forth, but it is necessary. Start by advising the group that there isn't a date that all will agree upon. You will need to go with the date that's best for the majority of people in the organizing committee. There will also be neighbors that cannot participate on the date you've selected. There's nothing you can do about that. Typically, the group will want to choose a holiday weekend. That's smart, but flawed too, a lot of households go away for the holiday. Also, consider that the local government may push back on holiday weekends as I mentioned in the case of my neighborhood on Independence Day, there may be limitations in access and resources. This is where having a neighbor who works for the local government can be very helpful. Still, if the group wants a holiday, don't dissuade them, but get a least two back up dates. There are several reasons for this:

1. You'll need the alternative dates in case local government refuses your first date
2. You'll need alternative dates due to weather
3. You'll need alternative dates based on participation

Make sure your local government committee (LGC) knows the preferred date and the alternate dates for their discussion with officials.

PARTICIPATING NEIGHBORS LIST

Next organize a subset committee to take on door-to-door neighbor sign up. This committee should be LARGE. You'll need as many people as possible because they will be going door-to-door and people should go in groups of three. You'll need bi-lingual people in each group of three. A minimum of 9 people on this committee is good. The reason for this is to ease the burden on everyone. If three people have to go to

60 homes and apartments, it's going to be too much work and you'll lose them. If it's broken up between 9 or 12, the workload is easier.

This committee will be in charge of signing up participating neighbors. They will go with clipboards and signup sheets. It's important that the NEIGHBOR sign their name on the signup sheet. The committee member should not write down anything on the sheet. The neighbor themselves should write their name, address and sign it. There's nothing official about it, but it will feel to them as if they've made an official commitment and decreases the possibility of them flaking on you. It's not a guarantee, it just gives you better odds.

Most importantly, this committee should: 1) set out on the sign up at least a month before the event, 2) the committee should NOT set out before the approval of the local government has been secured.

The committee should have a leader that is ok with giving their phone number to neighbors for questions, concerns or assistance. This person will be the point-of–contact for neighbors and the larger group and will have the list of participating neighbors. As people add or subtract from the list of participation, this person will control the master list. The master list is important as the team will use it for advertising and map creation.

COMMUNICATION AND ADVERTISING

Communication and advertising should be a sub-committee and have at least 3 members but no more than 5 unless you're planning a large signage campaign. The sub-committee is responsible for signage, digital or online advertising and will work with the leader of the participating neighbor committee to produce the participating family map.

The sub-committee will prepare an advertising plan to share with the larger committee. The sub-committee is solely responsible for the plan. Those not on the committee can ask for revisions to the plan, but must accept the final plan when completed.

The plan should include:

- ❏ Details of where physical signage will be located
    - o Will participating neighbors get signs?
    - o Signage locations on main thoroughfares
    - o Signage at local business
- ❏ Details of digital advertising
    - o Website & app ads
    - o Digital advertising on local government website
- ❏ Possible monetary or budget concerns

You can organize a neighborhood sale without it costing anything. If you have the right people on the right committee and they can think creatively about signage and are great political talkers, it's entirely possible. But you should consider the possibility that there will be a need for a budget and where that money will come from.

Before anyone takes out a checkbook, exhaust every idea. With regards to signage, as an example, on our main street in my little town, there is a business that does signs amongst other things. They produce t-shirts and ship packages as well. A partnership with them would be a very wise move. Then it's a matter of determining what you can give them in return for them producing the signage for them.

Obviously not everyone will have a local signage place, but you will have local business, so have the committee brainstorm ideas of how to get the local business to participate and perhaps donate or "sponsor" if money is really required.

I strongly encourage you to think creatively as much as possible. I've put several ideas, particularly on the topic of signage, in this book that won't cost you a dime. Still I understand that there may be costs that you simply can't avoid, particularly with regards to the local government and permits. I'll dive deeper into that shortly.

The advertising sub-committee cannot implement any plan without the approval and authorization of the larger committee. The larger committee cannot give final approval without the authorization of local government; therefore, the local government & the advertising sub-committees must work together to get an approved advertising plan. The local government sub-committee will present the advertising plan to the appropriate official(s) and get either their approval or changes. The advertising sub-committee should have a representative on the LGC for the purposes of attending any meetings that may be required by local government to get their approval, including town council meetings. This will aid in speeding the change/approval process.

Why is this necessary? Well the digital advertising is not of a concern to local government, but the physical signage itself is. Where signs are placed are subject to rules and therefore you will need a plan and preferably a map with defined places you want to place your signage. Visual aids are very helpful when speaking with local officials. Also, take pictures of the locations referred to on the maps. If possible, show plans of the signs themselves. Try to avoid actually making signs until you have approval from the officials.

In addition, you want to be able to count on local government to help you advertise. They can distribute maps, put something on their website, include the event on their town calendar/newsletter. Local government buy-in at every step in the organizing process is critical. Without it, do yourself a favor and stop.

Local Business Buy-in

Local business can be very helpful in pulling off a successful sale. If you can make them active participants in the planning, perhaps even add them to the committee in some capacity, you should. Local business already has connections with local government, so they can be a good resource for insight, if nothing else.

They can help in advertising by putting signs in their windows, messages on their marquees or just space for your planning meetings.

Of course, they are going to want something in return. Perhaps they should do it as a goodwill gesture to the neighborhood itself, but I wouldn't count on it. Consider how they can profit from the sale. If it's a restaurant, can they set up a stand or somehow provide refreshment to the visitors? If it's a barber or hair stylist, can they do haircuts in front of a non-participating but supportive neighbor's house?

Brainstorm with the larger committee to discuss how they can participate and what approval will be needed. Then, perhaps get a sub-committee devoted to local business buy in.

Local business buy in isn't critical to your plan or the sale. If this isn't something you have the resources for or you cannot gain the interest of the businesses, you can proceed without them. It's helpful, but not essential.

LARGER PURPOSE SALE

The larger purpose sale is a method by which you can have the sale serve as a way to donate to a charity, cause or neighborhood project. This can be a spectacular way to build neighborhood unity, get things done or just support something or someone you value.

It may not be that easy, you're asking for people to sell their stuff in order to give that money to something other than themselves, but people are generally pretty generous and will help a worthwhile project. Also, if you're getting push-back from your local authorities on permission for the sale, they might look more favorably if the sale was to benefit a neighborhood project or local charity.

If your committee does want to do have proceeds go to a charity, be sure to get that charity on board with it and provide your committee with a representative that can assist with any legal or tax implications. If the charity takes care of that end of things, the committee can be freed up to focus on other areas of the planning.

Getting neighbors to agree to donations may be something more of a challenge. The Participating Neighbor Committee will have to communicate the plan but more importantly the need. If neighbors feel invested in the cause, they are more likely to sign up. The committee won't be able to just show up at their door and ask them if they want to sell their stuff and give the money to your organizing committee. It's a harder sell, but tell the neighbor the story and chances are they'll want to help.

I personally think a charity or project is a great idea for a sale. It helps bond the community. Local government is much more likely to support your plan and it helps an organization or project get much needed funds. But it won't always work and you'll need to be savvy. It will also take some extra effort so, be sure this is the way to go before taking it on.

AFTER SALE CLEAN-UP

The after-sale cleanup is a critical piece of the planning process although it may seem like an afterthought. Your local government will have this top-of-mind and if you have a plan in place, you'll ease their concerns and be that much closer to securing their approval.

Form a sub-committee, perhaps of those neighbors who can't really devote time to the other committees due to their schedules, that will devise a plan for the clean-up. There will be a lot that goes unsold, unless they read this book (wink), and you will need to have a method to remove it.

HOW TO GET RID OF ALL THE JUNK

The sub-committee should have its own ideas for the clean up plan, but here are some thoughts:

1) Neighborhood Junkers: There are people in every community that go around and collect junk. You'll find them on trash day. They drive by, typically in pick-up trucks, and look for items that are either recyclable or can be resold. Connect with these

people and advise them of the plan. Ask if they can assist with clean up. Get phone numbers.

2) Partner with your trash collection company. Our company is Groot and they are very willing to work with the neighborhood on special "clean-up" projects. We typically have two: Spring & Fall clean-ups. They don't charge anything extra for this. In your case, ask the company what can be worked out and when it can be done in relation to the date(s) you've selected for your sale. They may insist on a cost for the special pick-up. This is where your negotiating skills come in handy. Emphasize the community spirit or if you are going to donate proceeds to a charity or project, make sure they know this and that should go a long way in getting them to participate. If all-else fails, ask if they would be willing to donate a roll-off dumpster or if they would be willing to waive the fees of your volunteers dropping off the refuse themselves.

It can be extremely helpful to engage your contact from government to assist in the conversations with the garbage collection company. They will know whom to talk to and quite possibly what will and will not work.

3) Neighborhood thrift stores are also a good resource for the leftovers. If there is a Goodwill or ReStore attempt to partner with them to have them pick up the leftovers. If they cannot pick up the items, you will have to drop them off.

This sub-committee should have people that have vehicles! Preferably, pick-up trucks or at the very least, vans. If you cannot get cooperation from the charities, garbage disposal or Junkers, you will need to dispose of the items yourself.

Don't get nervous, it's not that big of a deal. You'll simply have your team collect the leftovers, sort them into: 1) donations for Goodwill (or the like), metal recycling, waste management.

- Sort what can go to thrift stores, objects that are still usable but weren't sold. Clothes, knick-knacks, furniture, TVs, misc. objects
- Metal objects: these are items that aren't sold but could be sent to the recyclers for a little extra cash. (very little, don't get excited) Typically, your Junker crew will take care of this, but if they don't or you cannot muster them, this can be achieved by the sub-committee team. Find a recycling location nearby. You can ask your local waste management company or search the internet for their location. To encourage the committee, advise them that they can keep the money they get.
- Waste management: the rest of it, as I refer to it, will be just garbage. You'll know it when you see it. It's the stuff you can't imagine anyone would even bother putting out for a sale. It will be items that won't fall into the other categories. Now what you do with these items can be daunting. Hopefully, you can work something out with your waste management company that won't cost you anything. If you bring it to the waste management company, they will tend to work with you on costs.   I would encourage you to keep this portion to a minimum. If you think there is any possible way that an item can be used, consider it for the charity or "Goodwill" pile. The sub-committee should be prepared with garbage bags and willing to include it in their regular garbage pick-up.

- One final tip: Consider getting a roll-off. The waste management company will help you with this. It will cost money. If you are getting on with your waste management company, they may cut you a deal on it. If your sale is for a charity or project, they may even donate a roll off, but if they don't, try to negotiate the best possible deal. The reason a roll-off is such a great option is that if you do have a lot of garbage that just won't fit in the other categories, the roll-off dumpster will need to be located in a place where the sub-committee can drop off the garbage they collect. It may require someone with a large driveway or space for the roll-off. For very large neighborhood sales, the roll-off going to be a must.

LET'S TALK FUNDING

At this point, if you haven't already decided to drop the whole idea, you're thinking, "No way is this going to get done for free." That's entirely possible. I won't tell you it's not going to cost anything. It will cost you a lot in time and effort and sleep. But it also could require actual cash. So how do we manage this?

Wherever and whenever possible, if someone is requiring you to come up with cash, turn and walk away. There is always another way around an obstacle and cash can be a big obstacle. I have found in doing this a few times, that once you start doling out money, you find everyone has their hand out. It's almost like opening a faucet.

If a restaurant in your neighborhood, as an example, doesn't want to advertise your sale on their marquee without a payment, you have a few options: 1) pay the fee, 2) don't pay the fee and don't advertise there or 3) offer them something in return. I suggest offering to have your committees meet there exclusively. Advise the committee(s) that they should have their meetings at the restaurant and buy food. This is just an example, but my point is there's more than one way around an issue. Thinking creatively is key here. There is no reason you should have to reach in to your pocket if there is any way to avoid it.

Now, where you may not have an option is when dealing with the local government. They may require permits, application fees or whatever else they can think of. Getting them to waive these fees should not be a big deal. But what if it is? In my neighborhood the permit fee is $2 for a garage sale, but if 50 families sign up to participate in the neighborhood sale, that's $100. Where does that money come from? What if some families drop out? What if you don't know who will be participating or not? In this case, you could 1) collect money at the time a family signs up 2) start a collection amongst the committee 3) forget the whole thing. I would lean toward option three if your local authorities can't work with you on permit costs. Honestly, they are being short-sighted and that can be a difficult hurdle to climb and the permit process is just one of a thousand things the local government will need to work with you on. But let's say you're made of stronger stuff than I am and are ready to fight city hall. You may want to discuss with the committee the idea of getting sponsorship.

Sponsorship is a great way of getting funding when all else fails. Your sponsors will be the local businesses in the neighborhood. Grocery stores, restaurants, liquor stores, small business are all options for sponsors. As always, they'll want to know what's in it for them. You can appeal to their civic pride. Frankly, the neighborhood should know the businesses that support the community and the ones that don't and this is a great way to find out. For some businesses, you could suggest that they participate in the sale somehow. A grocery store, for example, can put some items out in front of their store for sale. A restaurant might have a sale of take away menu items or drinks to provide refreshment to Sale-ers. A boutique could have a sidewalk sale of their own. All this would require permits as well so the idea would be that the committee will plead their case as well as that of the neighborhood if the businesses pay the required fees.

There is always a way to get something done and people are generous, but they also have a great deal of pride in where they live. Even in some of the yuckier neighborhoods in my beloved Chicago, if you mention how yucky it is, you could be in for a fight. Lean on that pride. The idea with a neighborhood sale is not just about making money, getting rid of your junk, recycling or whatever, it's about the community united. It's about pride in where you live and how great it is. It boosts home values when a community comes together. People want to live where there is a good, solid community and there's no better way to build that community than having events like a neighborhood sale or block party. Use this argument with your local government as well as local business to encourage them to support rather than obstruct the plan.

NEIGHBORHOOD GARAGE SALE WRAP PARTY

The work involved in getting a neighborhood sale together is tremendous. To continue the community feeling and the bonds you've manage to build over this odyssey, consider having a thank you party for the committees. It's important to thank these people for all the work put in. It doesn't have to cost a lot. Perhaps have it at a neighborhood restaurant sponsor or just have it at your place with pizza or spaghetti. Or just have everyone over for cake and coffee. It's about acknowledging the work that was done and the battle won. Then maybe talk about doing it again next year? (wink)

FINAL THOUGHTS FOR ORGANIZERS

Okay organizers, there are some things I want you to watch out for in your organizing. I've learned this over the years and I beg you to save yourself a lot of angst and hurt feelings and pay heed:

Know when to step OFF – You'll have a vision of how everything should go. Don't let the vision become a tyrant. You are not doing this all yourself. Other people have ideas and visions of their own. Be ready and WILLING to let go of your vision if the team prefers another. If you think something should be a certain way, but a committee member thinks otherwise and they are willing to see it through, bonus, less work for you.

There are going to be moments where you see your committee or sub-committee going sideways. If you are not asked for assistance, stay out of it. Don't jump in and fix anything or anyone. Keep your role as organizer or lead or whatever you call yourself, as light a touch as possible. Micro-managing is a good way to lose volunteers. The committees will have disagreements, arguments or maybe even a knock-down drag out fight, don't get involved unless it's absolutely necessary. People will quit, flake or just be lousy at their jobs. It's totally okay. This is a learning experience for all. Trust your committee leads. Let them do their jobs to the best of their ability.

The end result of this project will not look like what you envisioned. That's totally okay and you must be totally okay with that. Remember, it's not about you.

Your most important job as organizer is to keep it fun. If this turns into an unpaid job for your committees, your sale won't be successful. Remember to keep it light and when you see your team stressing, help them to de-stress. Maybe it's a cup of tea or a beer. Maybe it's just sitting them down and letting them vent or maybe they just need a big bear hug. Get them smiling again by telling them a joke. That's your most important role as a leader. It is a lot of work, but it should be fun work, you can make it fun.

I hope you find your way through the weeds of the neighborhood sale and this chapter gets you over some of the bumps. You have to be stout of heart and a bit nuts to take it on, but we sale-ers have all the right stuff to get it done and have a blast doing it. Best of luck to you and please get in touch to let me know how it goes.

ONE LAST THING...

If you enjoyed this book or found it useful I'd be very grateful if you'd post a short review on Amazon. Your support really does make a difference and I read all the reviews personally so I can get your feedback and make this book even better.

Thanks again for your support! Happy Sale-ing!!!!!